ENCOUNTERS
WITH
CHRIST

Experience the Miracles and
Transforming Power of
an Unexpected Savior

RICHARD EXLEY

WHITE STONE BOOKS
LAKELAND, FLORIDA

Published in association with Yates & Yates, LLP, Attorneys and Counselors, Orange, California

09 08 07 06   9 8 7 6 5 4 3 2 1

Encounters with Christ:
Experience the Miracles and Transforming Power of an Unexpected Savior

ISBN 1-59379-025-2
Copyright © 2005 by Richard Exley
P.O. Box 54744
Tulsa, Oklahoma 74155

Published by White Stone Books, Inc.
P.O. Box 2835
Lakeland, Florida 33806

DEDICATION

To him who is able to keep you from falling
and to present you before his glorious presence
without fault and with great joy—
to the only God our Savior
be glory, majesty, power and authority,
through Jesus Christ our Lord,
before all ages, now and forevermore!

Jude 1:24, 25

CONTENTS

TO THE READER

I first learned the great stories of Scripture as a child in Sunday school. One of the most effective teachers I ever had was a woman named LuElla Headly. She taught the beginners class of four and five year olds. Although our classroom was located in the church basement, in a musty area under the stairs, she had a way of transforming it into a vibrant learning center.

Her most effective teaching tool was the peep box. She created it by lining the inside of a shoe box with full-color scenes illustrating stories from the Bible. Next she took cutout figures of Bible characters and pasted them to the bottom of the box so they stood upright, creating a three-dimensional effect. Finally, she covered the top of the shoe box with white tissue paper.

Each week when I placed my eye against the half-dollar-sized peep hole in the end of that shoe box, I was transported into another time and place. No longer was I sitting in that musty room beneath the stairs. Now I was standing with Moses on Mount Sinai. I was with Isaiah in the temple. I was with Jesus in Gethsemane. In that moment, the great stories of the Bible came alive for me.

That is what I am praying will happen for you when you read *Encounters with Christ*. May it become a "peep box" transporting you to another time and place, to a time when real people with real problems encountered Jesus in a life-changing way.

Within the factual framework of Scripture, history, and tradition, I give my imagination free rein to create twelve vivid, first person vignettes. Each vignette is based on a familiar Bible story—the woman with an issue of blood, the man born blind, Nicodemus, and others. As you read these accounts, I believe that the stories you've known since childhood will come alive like never before. You may even have a fresh encounter with Christ.

Each vignette is complemented by a "Life Lesson" giving further insight into the spiritual principles involved. In addition, I will share examples of contemporary people who have experienced Christ in similar ways. You will meet Bob, the hard drinking crop duster who met Jesus in Lil's Cafe just off of Highway 50 in southeastern Colorado. Then there's Charlotte whose dead thyroid was healed following an encounter with Jesus at church one Sunday morning. And there's JJ and Tracy Woodie who were told that they would never be able to have children of their own.

They experienced the Lord's healing touch at a camp meeting in Oklahoma and now they are the proud parents of two beautiful children.

Encounters with Christ is more than just a book to be read. It is an invitation to experience Christ in all His fullness for yourself. If you are ill, may you encounter the Healer. If you are in bondage to fear or addiction, may you encounter the One who comes to liberate the captives. If you have made some unwise decisions or lost your way, may you encounter the One who comes to seek and save the lost. If you are feeling overwhelmed, even discouraged, may you encounter the One whose presence will renew your faith and warm your heart. If you are a worshipper, may you encounter the object of your devotion. Wherever you are in life, I pray that you may be refreshed, restored, and renewed as you encounter Christ anew!

Richard Exley
Emerald Pointe, Arkansas

CHAPTER ONE

The Daughter of Jairus

Luke 8:40-55

LOOKING OUT THE SMALL WINDOW, I search the sky over Capernaum for the first hint of daylight. Nothing. Not even a smudge of light on the eastern horizon. *Will this long night never end,* I wonder, as I retrace my steps across the room.

Her breathing is labored, her skin is flushed with fever, and her lips are cracked and dry. Lifting the stub of a candle I study her youthful features, searching for something of myself in her face. All I find is a younger version of her mother—the same high cheekbones and fair skin. Looking at her now, my heart hurts.

She is only twelve years old and the last of our children. Being the only girl she is dear to me, which makes her mysterious illness even more disconcerting. Neither medicine nor prayer has proved effective, making me nearly mad with fear.

The best physicians in Capernaum are as mystified as her mother and me. She has eaten nothing for two days, and she is nearly incoherent with fever. From time to time she rouses herself to take a sip of water or a little juice, but that is all. What began as a headache and a slight fever has progressed over the past few days until we now fear for her life.

Never have I felt so helpless, and a strange feeling it is for a man of my stature. I am the ruler of the local synagogue, a position of no little importance. In our community, I am known as a man who gets things done, but against her illness I can do nothing. I am powerless to ease her suffering or to make her whole.

A painful groan escapes her cracked lips and I move to comfort her. Gently, I cool her feverish brow with a damp cloth. Carefully, I spoon a few drops of water into her mouth, willing her to swallow it. When she is still, I give myself to my tormented thoughts once more.

Though I am a religious man, I am tempted to rage at the Almighty. Why should my daughter suffer so; she is an innocent. What wrongs could one so young commit to deserve such a fate? And if she is suffering for my sins or the sins of her mother, that hardly seems just. What kind of God would allow such a thing?

Of course, I do not utter such thoughts lest I be guilty of blasphemy. The last thing I want to do is to bring judgment upon my family.

Retreating to the couch beneath the window on the far wall, I search for an answer, for a way to help this daughter of mine. Almost against my will, my thoughts turn to the Teacher who is known as Jesus of Nazareth. It is said that He now resides in Capernaum, though I know not where. He is a controversial figure to be sure. Many of the common people think He is a prophet, but most of my colleagues think He is a fraud.

I don't know what to think about Him. Were it not for the predicament in which I now find myself, I would probably dismiss Him out of hand. Prophet or lunatic it would matter little to me. But with my daughter's life hanging in the balance, I find I am willing to consider almost any option. Maybe He really can heal the sick. Maybe He can heal my precious daughter, the light of my life.

It is a risky path I am considering. I cannot approach Jesus without risking the disapproval of my colleagues. They despise Him and think by ignoring Him that He will go away. I am an influential man in the synagogue—should

I approach Him, it will give credibility to His ministry. My actions will anger the teachers of the Law, of that I am sure.

Yet, if I don't seek His help, my daughter may very well die. Of what use would the goodwill of the religious leaders, be if I do nothing and she is taken from me? Of course Jesus may be a fraud, duping the simpleminded. If that is the case, I will have risked my reputation for nothing.

Around and around go my anxious thoughts, leaving me exhausted but no nearer a decision. Burying my face in my hands, I find I am weeping in fear and frustration. If only I knew what to do. If only I knew…

Sleep must have overtaken me because when I awaken, bright bars of sunlight are streaming through the window and into the room. For a moment I am disoriented and I can make no sense of my surroundings. With an effort I will my sleep-drugged mind to function. Slowly the room comes into focus and I see my wife bending over our daughter. At first her touch is gentle, her words soothing, but then she grows frantic.

"Wake up," she says. "Wake up!"

Her shrill words jerk me fully awake and I lunge across the room to stand beside her. Frantically, I survey the situation, noting that our daughter is breathing, though with great effort. She is obviously unconscious and not responding to my wife's desperate attempts to arouse her.

In an instant I know what I must do. I must find Jesus. He is our only hope. I only pray I have not waited too long.

Turning on my heel I rush toward the door, calling over my shoulder to my wife as I exit the room.

Once in the street I pause, not sure where to look for Him. Desperately I try to recall any tidbit of information I may have heard that could offer some clue to His whereabouts. Maybe something one of the servants said, or a fragment of conversation overheard in the synagogue—anything to point me in the right direction.

Someone said a few of His closest followers were fishermen; at least I think I remember something to that effect.

In an instant I know what I must do. I must find Jesus.

Brothers, I think. It's little enough to go on, but at least it gives me a place to start. Quickly I head toward the waterfront. Maybe someone on the lake will know where I can find Him.

Turning a final corner, I see the lake sparkling in the morning light. More importantly a large crowd has gathered. The excitement is palpable and my heart leaps within me. Hurriedly I force my way through the throng, too desperate to be polite. My daughter's life is at stake and I must find Jesus.

He is standing with His back to the lake, a small boat beached a few steps away. Though I have never seen Him, I know it is He. There is nothing physically impressive about Him, yet I find myself drawn to Him. He has a certain magnetism, an inner energy unlike anything I have ever experienced.

Now that I have found Him I'm not sure how to approach Him. Nervously I search the crowd. As I feared, some of the more critical teachers of the Law are here. They are huddled together exhibiting a thinly veiled disdain. I am well-known to them, and I have little doubt that they will make much to-do about my being here. Still, that is of little concern to me now. At this moment all I care about is my daughter's well-being.

Jesus is looking my way, as if He senses my desperation, and His eyes are full of compassion. Pushing through the last of the crowd, I rush forward and fall at His feet, imploring Him, "Teacher, my daughter is desperately ill. She is dying. Please come and lay Your hands upon her. Heal her and restore her life."

Taking me by the arm, He helps me to my feet. "Take Me to her," He says, falling into step beside me.

Instantly the crowd surrounds us, pressing close. Everyone, it seems, is eager to see a miracle. Remembering my daughter's deathly pale face and labored breathing, I try to pick up the pace, but it is no use. The crowd has a mind of its own and it will not be hurried.

Suddenly Jesus stops. Turning around He surveys the throng. "Who touched Me?" He asks. "Who touched My clothes?"

I am stunned. Why has He stopped? Doesn't He realize that we have no time to waste? My daughter's life is hanging in the balance!

Glancing at Him in disbelief one of the disciples says, "You are surrounded by people. The crowd is jostling You. What do You mean, 'Who touched Me?'"

My sentiments exactly!

Still searching the crowd, Jesus replies, "This touch was different. I felt healing virtue go out of Me."

Though I am nearly beside myself, Jesus will not be hurried. I bite my tongue to keep from saying something I may regret, while tears of frustration momentarily blind me. In my mind's eye, all I can see is my wife bending over the nearly lifeless body of our beloved daughter.

An audible murmur sweeps the crowd and in spite of myself, I lift my eyes. As if by magic the throng parts and a woman, trembling with fear, falls at His feet. Kneeling, Jesus takes both of her hands in His and looks her in the eye.

"What is it?" He asks.

"I am the one who touched You," she says, in a voice I have to strain to hear. "I was desperate. I had nowhere else to turn. For twelve years I have been sick. I have no idea how many doctors I have seen. Too many, I can assure You! And not one of them has been able to help me.

"I had lost all hope, but then I saw You and something leaped within my heart. I just knew that if I could touch Your clothes, I would be healed."

Helping her to her feet He says, "Daughter, your faith has healed you. Go in peace and be free from your suffering."

I am amazed at her transformation. She looks so different now. Her face is radiant and her eyes are sparkling. As she moves back into the crowd there is a bounce in her step. Just before the crowd swallows her, she turns toward Jesus one last time and when she does, her face is full of love.

My heart is singing. For the first time in days I dare to hope, I dare to believe that my own daughter will be restored to us. If that chronically ill woman could be healed by simply touching His clothes, then surely there is nothing He cannot do.

"Jairus."

Turning I find myself face-to-face with my chief servant, the steward in charge of my house. One look at his face and I know something is wrong, terribly wrong!

My daughter is dead!

He doesn't have to tell me. I can see the tragic truth in his eyes.

"Don't bother the Teacher anymore," he says. "Let's go home. Your wife needs you."

He takes my arm and numbly I turn to follow him.

Suddenly Jesus is beside me, His hand on my arm. His face is full of compassion and in His eyes there burns an intense light. "Don't be afraid," He says, "just believe."

I am too dazed to respond and before I know it, we are approaching my home. Already the professional mourners have gathered, their mournful cry and the wail of their flutes a fitting dirge, for the light of my life is gone. Her young life snuffed out before it hardly began.

Entering my home Jesus raises His hands for silence. As the grief-stricken wails slowly subside, I move to my wife's side. Burying her face in my shoulder she sobs softly, a sound so sad I am sure she has suffered a wound from which she will never recover. Nor will I, for like her, I loved our daughter more than life itself.

"Why all this commotion and wailing?" Jesus asks, His resonate voice filling the wide room where we have gathered. "The child is not dead, she is only sleeping."

Instantly derisive laughter echoes around the room.

Someone calls out, "How can You say she is sleeping when You haven't even seen her?"

Another says, "She is dead! Of that you may be sure."

He nods toward His three followers and they begin moving the mourners outside. When the room is empty except for my wife, and me, and His three disciples, He motions for us to follow Him.

Stepping into the small room where our daughter's body is laid out, I nearly gag with grief. A hoard of regrets wash over me. If only I had sought His help sooner. If only I had not been so proud, so stubborn. If only…

I sense Him looking at me and though it is hard, I force myself to look Him in the eye. My own sorrow is mirrored there, and I take what comfort I can from His compassion. Yet, there is something else there too—a righteous indignation, a kind of holy hatred. I fear sickness and death, but He despises them.

"Don't be afraid," He says again, "just believe."

My wife is trembling as I am. Putting my arm around her shoulder, I draw her close. Together we watch as Jesus takes the hand of our only daughter, now cold and still in death.

For a moment He does nothing; then He speaks in a voice full of love. "Precious child, I say to you, get up!"

Instantly her eyelids flutter and her chest heaves. My wife screams and I think she is going to faint. My heart is hammering in my chest and I can hardly breathe.

Now our beloved child is sitting up and looking around. When her eyes find me, she smiles with delight. "Abba, father," she cries, reaching for me.

Jumping up from the bed, she flings herself into our arms. I am laughing and crying, while her mother covers her face with kisses.

"You're alive!" my wife says in stunned disbelief, hardly able to believe what has happened.

Holding her at arm's length, she looks at our daughter in amazement. "It's a miracle! You're a miracle! You were dead, but now look at you. You're alive!"

Once more the three of us embrace, and then we are whirling about the room delirious with joy. When at last we collapse from exhaustion, panting for breath, I think of Jesus. Where is He? Has He slipped away?

No. There He is, off to one side watching us with an amused expression on His face, His eyes dancing with joy.

Breaking away from my wife and daughter, I make my way to Him. For the second time today, I find myself kneeling at His feet. Not in petition this time, but in praise and thanksgiving. Humbly I worship Him, pouring out my love and gratitude in words that seem far too small for what I feel.

Though life gradually falls back into a familiar routine, I often find myself thinking of Him, especially when I try to imagine what our lives would have been like had He not come when He did. There is much I still do not understand. There are those who believe He is the Son of God. Others discredit this, pointing out that He is the son of a deceased carpenter named Joseph, and that His mother and brothers are well-known. What I believe regarding such things I am not sure, but this one thing I do know. My daughter, who was dead, is now alive. If He is not God's Son, how do I explain that?

Life Lessons

LIFE LESSONS

The Daughter of Jairus

IF YOUR CHILD HAS EVER been seriously ill, you can undoubtedly identify with Jairus. If you've ever heard the doctor say, "We are doing all we can, but things don't look good," you know what I am talking about. At times like that, it matters little whether you are a person of power and influence or just an average Joe. Humanly speaking, there is nothing you can do except maintain your silent vigil. Never will you feel more helpless, more inadequate.

Our journey to death's door started when our daughter developed a low-grade fever followed by vomiting. She was only eight months old and by the third day, she appeared dehydrated. Belatedly we decided to take her to the pediatrician's office. After examining her, he gave her an injection of penicillin. Instantly she went into convulsions, her tiny body rigid with spastic contractions.

Quickly the doctor ordered a second injection to control her convulsions. When it failed to stop the seizures, he ordered a third, which also proved futile. By now Brenda and I were nearly beside ourselves. Any illusions we had about the seriousness of the situation were shattered when the doctor scooped Leah's rigid body into his arms and ran for his car. Brenda and his nurse followed and in seconds we were racing for the hospital.

I rushed after them in my own car, fear pushing me ever closer to the point of panic. It seemed that all I could see was Leah's tiny body, rigid and spastic, her eyes rolled back in her head. Would I ever see her smile again, or hear her giggle contentedly as Brenda pinned a dry diaper on her freshly powdered bottom?

Terrifying thoughts of death—Leah's death, our baby's death—tried to take control of my mind. With a Herculean effort, I dismissed them only to have them return a minute later and with a vengeance. There were other thoughts too, almost as terrifying—Leah, brain-damaged or growing up afflicted with epilepsy.

I skidded to a stop in the hospital parking lot just in time to see the doctor rush Leah into a specially equipped emergency area. For the next two-and-one-half hours, the doctors worked to save her life. Brenda and I were left alone to await the outcome. In desperation I called my family and Brenda's, begging them to pray. Distinctly I can recall the desolation that washed over me after I placed the telephone receiver on the hook. Standing beside the now silent phone, at the end of the empty hallway, I felt totally alone.

After getting hold of myself, I made my way back to where Brenda was nervously pacing the floor just outside the emergency area. We clung to each other and cried and prayed. Together we faced the harsh reality—Leah might not live, and if she did, she might never be the same again. Never had life seemed so empty of hope, so crowded with pain and fear. Yet even as we came to grips with the terrifying possibility of Leah's death and all that would mean to us, we also began to sense God's presence. In our spirits it seemed we heard Him say, "Don't be afraid; just believe."[1]

The possibility of Leah's death was not diminished, it was no less real; yet in a way that defies explanation, we were suddenly at peace. We did not overcome our fear by minimizing the seriousness of Leah's condition, for that would have been nothing more than foolish denial. Instead, we focused on His words. Not just Luke 8:50, but many other passages as well. Passages like Mark 10:27, "With man this is impossible, but not with God; all things are possible with God." And Matthew 17:20, "I tell you the truth, if you have faith as small as a mustard seed, you can say to this mountain, 'Move from here to there' and it will move. Nothing will be impossible for you."

After nearly three hours, the doctor finally emerged from the emergency area, looking exhausted but relieved. "Your baby is out of danger," he informed us, "she is going to live." He wanted her to stay in the hospital for a few more days. There were a number of tests he wanted to run. He listened patiently as we bombarded him with a host of questions and concerns. After answering as best he could, he excused himself and we were left alone once again.

Only we weren't alone—Jesus was with us! As surely as ever He was with Jairus, He was present in that hospital with us. Not in physical form, but just as real. And from Him we drew the strength and courage to face whatever the future might hold.

Just then, Leah was wheeled out of the emergency area and Brenda gasped. She was clothed only in a diaper, her hands and feet were fastened to the rungs of the crib with cloth cords, and an IV was flowing into a vein in her head. We followed as the nurse took her into the nursery. For a long time we simply stood beside her tiny bed watching her sleep, relieved somehow just by the gentle motion of her breathing. The storm wasn't over, but the crisis had passed, at least for the moment, and I found myself overwhelmed with gratefulness to God.

Like Jairus, we turned to Jesus in the hour of our trial, when Leah's life hung by a slender thread, and He did not fail us. Not only did He spare her life, but He completely healed her, as well. Although the doctors put her through a battery of tests over the next several weeks, they could find no abnormalities. She is now thirty-five years old and she has never suffered another seizure.

If someone you love is desperately ill and in need of healing, do what Jairus did—go to Jesus. Like Jairus, you may have to risk the ridicule of your friends. You may have to lay aside your pride and humble yourself before the Lord. You may even have to risk making a fool out of yourself in your own eyes, but that is a small price to pay for your loved one's healing. Remember, "'God opposes the proud but gives grace to the humble.' Humble yourselves, therefore, under God's mighty hand, that he may lift you up in due time. Cast all your anxiety on him because he cares for you."[2]

CHAPTER TWO

A Desperate Woman

Mark 5:25-34

ALTHOUGH IT IS STILL EARLY, a crowd is gathering. Through the small window above my bed, I can hear the murmur of voices and the rush of feet. *What is it now,* I wonder, as I push myself erect. A wave of sickness rolls over me and for a moment I think I am going to faint. When it passes I pull myself to my feet. Leaning against the wall, I try to gather my strength. The simplest tasks— putting my clothes on, preparing breakfast, even eating— now leave me exhausted.

Moving outside, I sit on a small stool and lean my back against the wall. The sun is warm on my face. Closing my eyes I soak in its warmth.

Around me the noise of the city continues, but I hardly hear it. Rainbows of colored light dance behind my eyelids and I am a child again. We are playing in the garden, my sister and I. There is no sorrow there, just the running laughter of children. We are as carefree as the first barefoot day of spring. Suffering and disease are just words, something of which we have no knowledge.

Thinking of my sister, I experience a familiar ache. Though we were once close, it has been years since we have spoken. Sometimes I make my way to the market in hopes of catching sight of her. I go early and sit in the shadows against the wall. If she sees me, she pays me no mind. Although I am tempted to call to her, I never do. She obviously feels guilty, while I battle bouts of jealousy—hardly a recipe for a relationship.

What began as a nostalgic reprieve has now taken a sadistic turn. Although it is not unfamiliar, it never fails to catch me by surprise. With an effort I return to the present. The sun is still warm on my face but no longer pleasant. The bittersweet memories have tainted everything, even this sunlit morning.

Although I have little interest in the world around me, I cannot help but notice the excitement in the air. Throngs of people are hurrying past my tiny house. From my vantage point against the wall, I can feel their urgency. Now and then I catch a snatch of conversation.

"He did what?"

"He rebuked the storm and it stopped."

"You don't believe that do you?"

"What does it matter what I believe? I'm just telling you what I heard."

They turn the corner toward the waterfront, still arguing, and I am left to wonder who they could have been talking about. Not that it matters. The calming of a storm is of little interest to me.

A child's voice can be heard above the murmur of conversation. For a moment I am transfixed. A rush of emotions tug at my heart, a host of memories tempt me, but with an effort I resist. I am not going there. Though the memories promise comfort, experience has taught me that it is an empty promise.

Pushing myself to my feet, I wait for the dizziness to pass before going inside in search of my medicine. It is a foul concoction consisting of a powder compounded from rubber, alum, and garden crocuses mixed with a goblet of wine.[3] It is the last in a long line of treatments that were supposed to cure me, but haven't. For twelve years my condition has only grown worse. Still, since I have no other hope I force myself to drink all of it, nearly gagging before I get it down.

I have much to be thankful for, at least that is what I tell myself. It's how I get through these difficult days. Though my husband divorced me, he did not leave me destitute. He allows me to live in this small house, and if it were not for my medical bills, I could manage quite nicely. As it is I am nearly penniless. It probably doesn't matter, for I cannot live much longer. Day by day I feel my life ebbing out of me.

How this could have happened to me I do not know. I was always healthy. That is until I gave birth to my first child. Though the birth was not difficult as births go, I was never able to recover. As the weeks passed with no sign of improvement, I experienced a growing concern, but even then I was not alarmed. Whatever concern I may have had was soon forgotten in the joy of motherhood. Of course I was tired all of the time but, I reasoned, what mother of a newborn isn't?

Although my physical condition wore on me, the hardest part was being segregated, ostracized really. According to the Law of Moses, I was ceremonially unclean and anyone or anything I touched became unclean.[4] Of course I could not be intimate with my husband[5] nor could I worship in the Temple or in the synagogue.

When it became apparent that I wasn't going to be cured, my husband decided to divorce me. I begged him not to do it. I threatened to kill myself. I told him I would surely die if he took my son from me. It was all to no avail. My desperate pleas, my hysterical ranting, fell on deaf ears. His mind was made up.

I am weary with my reminiscing. No good can come of it. Even if I could figure out why things happened the way they did, it would not change one thing.

Once more I shuffle outside to reclaim my stool. As I am making myself comfortable, a throng of people turn the corner. In a matter of seconds, they have filled this narrow street. The crowd is made up mostly of ordinary people, shopkeepers and fishermen, with a sprinkling of women. Some of the religious leaders are present though they do not seem to share the crowd's exuberance. At the sight of them, I cringe involuntarily. Although they look my way, they do not seem to see me. To them I have no name. I am just a faceless woman with an incurable issue of blood. As far as they are concerned, I will be forever unclean.

As the crowd surges toward me, my attention is drawn to the Man in the forefront. He must be the cause of all of this excitement for the crowd presses close about Him. A dignified man with an anxious face takes Him by the elbow and tries to push his way through the throng, but it is no use. Turning toward the Man, he pleads with Him. Although I cannot hear what he is saying above the roar of voices, there is no mistaking his urgency. Now the crowd is abreast of me and their energy is palpable. It has a physical presence. I can feel it.

Above the furor I hear someone shouting, "Son of David…Son of David…" and my heart leaps. Could this ordinary looking Man be the Healer I have heard so much about? Is He the same One who cleansed the leper?[6] Is He the prophet who raised the son of the widow of Nain from the dead?[7]

Suddenly a wild and crazy thought fills my mind. *If He really is a prophet, if He really did heal the sick and raise the dead, then maybe He can heal me too.* Just as quickly, I push it from my mind. Why get my hopes up? Why would He have anything to do with a woman like me?

Despair settles upon me like a thick fog. Twelve years of suffering have taken their toll. Not just physically, but emotionally as well. I simply do not have the strength to hope again. I have already suffered too many broken dreams, too many false promises. Better to use what little strength I have left to cope with my sickness than to waste it chasing after a fantasy.

Still, try as I might, I cannot rid myself of this hope. It seems to have taken on a life of its own, no matter how irrational that may be. Besides, what do I have to lose? If I do nothing, I am going to die. Maybe, just maybe, this itinerant holy man can heal me.

Yielding to this desperate hope, I push myself to my feet and step into the street. Instantly the flow of the crowd carries me forward, and I find myself pushing ahead in an attempt to work my way closer to the Healer. Belatedly I realize that everyone I touch is now ceremonially unclean until evening. Well,

Could this ordinary looking Man be the Healer I have heard so much about?

there is nothing I can do about it now so with renewed determination I forge ahead.

Now that I have committed myself to this desperate hope, I find strength I did not know I had. With renewed energy I squirm through the throng, working my way ever closer. At last I am directly behind Him and a little to His left. I can almost touch Him. This is the moment of truth, the moment for which I have been waiting these past twelve years.

While fighting my way through the crowd, I became convinced that if I could just touch Him I would be healed. Yet, now that I am within arm's reach, something holds me back. Fear, I think. He is my last hope. What if I touch Him and nothing happens? What will I do then? Without hope I will surely die!

Pushing my fears aside, I lunge forward and grasp the tassel hanging from the corner of His garment. When I touch it, a surge of energy flows through my body. In an instant I am revitalized! Every trace of my long illness is gone. The weakness and the perpetual exhaustion have vanished. I haven't felt like this since I was a girl.

Although I can hardly contain my joy, I slip into the crowd hoping to escape unnoticed. I have not taken more than a step or two when His voice rings out, "Who touched My clothes?"

His closest disciples look at Him in amazement. Finally one of them says, "You see the people crowding against You and yet You can ask, 'Who touched Me?'"

Ignoring them, His eyes continue to search the crowd. I cover my face and slip behind a large man. It is no use, for I can still feel His eyes upon me. When I look up, He is staring at me. Those nearest Him follow His gaze, and I am now the center of attention. There is nothing to do but acknowledge what I have done and accept the consequences, whatever they may be.

The crowd parts and I slowly make my way toward Him. Trembling with fear I fall at His feet. With my face pressed to the ground, I wait for His reprimand, His rebuke. When He says nothing, I risk a glance at Him and see that His face is full of kindness.

Now I am weeping, not in sorrow, but tears of joy. I cannot even remember the last time someone looked at me with kindness. Pity, yes, and disgust, but not kindness. With a rush of words, I pour out my story, oblivious to the crowd which presses close to hear what I have to say for myself. I tell Him everything. Not just how I touched His garment and was instantly healed, but everything. I tell Him about my chronic illness and about being ostracized from my family because of my ceremonial uncleanness. I even tell Him how my husband divorced me and took my son from me.

When I finally stumble to a stop, He squats down and gently raises my chin so He can look me in the eye. "Daughter," He says, "your faith has healed you. Go in peace and be free from your suffering."

Taking my hand He helps me to my feet. Turning His attention back to the dignified gentleman, who has become grief stricken after receiving a message from the steward of his house, He says, "Don't be afraid; just believe." They move off together and the crowd follows, leaving me alone on the street.

For the first time in longer than I can remember, I am free from the weight of my illness—not only the physical symptoms I have suffered, but the heaviness of grief that I have carried all these years. When He said, "Go in peace…" I felt the anger and bitterness drain out of me and the sorrow, too. Turning toward home I find that I am thinking about the future rather than the past, about what awaits me rather than what I have lost. More than anything I am thinking about the Prophet whose healing touch gave new life to me.

"Don't be afraid; just believe."

Life Lessons

A Desperate Woman

ALTHOUGH WE KNOW ALMOST NOTHING about her, that this was a desperate woman is obvious enough. Mark's Gospel tells us that she had been ill with an issue of blood for twelve years.[8] Not only was she weakened by her chronic anemia, but she probably had to battle ever increasing bouts of loneliness, even depression. The Levitical law[9] required her to be segregated from the company of worshippers as long as her condition continued. That was difficult enough, but by the time of Jesus, the rabbis had added their own traditions and requirements. According to rabbinical interpretation, cases such as hers were always the result of personal sin. "Moreover, by the law of the rabbis, for the same cause she was divorced from her husband, and shut out from family life. All this inevitably meant that she was ostracized by society."[10] Little wonder that she was desperate.

If you are struggling with a terminal disease or even a chronic illness, you can probably identify with her, at least in part. Even though you have not been segregated from your family, it may feel like you have been abandoned.

While your family and friends are attentive to your physical needs, they will likely try to avoid any discussion regarding your illness or possible death.

Perhaps you have tried to talk about your feelings. Maybe you said something like, "I don't have much to look forward to anymore," or something even more direct: "I think I am going to die soon," only to have them respond by changing the subject. Worse yet they may have said, "Don't talk like that. You're going to live for years. Why, you'll probably outlive me."

While their conscious intent may have been to encourage you, you were hardly encouraged. Instead, you felt isolated, left to face your sickness and death alone.

When a person is ill with a nonfatal disease, a nurse may restrict visitors to encourage bed rest. When the diagnosis is "terminal," people begin withdrawing voluntarily. It has been observed that some people initially have close contact with their terminally ill loved ones such as hugging them or kissing them on the lips. Then they begin to give a good-bye or hello kiss on the forehead, then the hand, and finally they simply blow a kiss from across the room. Tragically, the patient gets the message.

Unlike the rabbis of Jesus' day, we do not believe that chronic illness is necessarily an indication of personal sin nor do we consider it grounds for divorce, nevertheless many marriages fail under the weight of illness. Well-known author Philip Yancey tells of a thirty-three-year-old friend who discovered he had one of the rarest, most severe forms of cancer. In medical history, only twenty-seven people were known to have been treated for this precise form of cancer. The other twenty-six patients were dead.

At his friend's request, Yancey began accompanying him to a therapy group at a nearby hospital. The group consisted of people who were dying; most of them were in their thirties.

Yancey writes, "I was most affected by the one elderly person in the room, a handsome, gray-haired woman with the broad, bony face of an Eastern European immigrant. She expressed her loneliness in simple sentences veiled in a thick accent. We asked if she had any family. An only son was trying to get emergency leave from the air force in Germany. And her husband? She swallowed hard a few times and then said, 'He came to see me just once. I was in the hospital. He brought me my bathrobe and a few things. The doctor stood in the hallway and told him about my leukemia.' Her voice started to crack, and she dabbed at her eyes before continuing. 'He went home that night, packed up all his things, and left. I never saw him again.'

"'How long had you been married?' I asked.

"Several people in the group gasped aloud at her answer: 'Thirty-seven years.'"[11]

Yancey concludes with a painful observation, "In this group of thirty people, no marriages remained intact longer than two years—including my friend Jim's."[12]

When I read Yancey's account, I found myself thinking not only of that elderly woman with the thick accent, but of this desperate woman with the issue of blood. Like her twentieth century counterpart, she was terribly ill and beyond the help of medical science. The Bible says, "She had suffered a great deal under the care of many doctors and had spent all she had, yet instead of getting better she grew worse."[13]

But that is not the end of her story, not by a long shot. If it were, we would probably have never heard of her. Instead of hanging onto her hurts and disappointments and turning into a prematurely old and bitter woman, she reached out to Jesus. Instead of slowly wasting away before finally succumbing to death, she took a chance, she risked making a fool of herself. She acted on her faith saying to herself, "If I just touch his clothes, I will be healed."[14]

And she was! "...she came up behind him in the crowd and touched his cloak...Immediately her bleeding stopped and she felt in her body that she was freed from her suffering."[15]

What Jesus did for her He can do for you! No matter how sick you are, no matter how hopeless your situation is, Jesus can heal you.

A few days ago I received a wonderful letter from a young mother for whom I had prayed. Enclosed with the letter was a picture of her husband, herself, and two beautiful children. This is what she wrote:

> My husband was told that he would never be able to father children naturally. That we would need extensive infertility treatments and there was still no guarantee that they would work. We had several tests run on him that confirmed this final diagnosis. You prophesied[16] over us that we would have "several" children and that it would be done in Jesus' name. My husband and I truly felt the confirmation of this and received it to the fullest extent! We stood on the Word of God during our time of struggle and believed in faith that God would provide this natural miracle (without any technological means).

I am happy to announce your prophecy is coming to pass! On September 3, 2002, I gave birth to a beautiful daughter, Gracie Abigail Woodie. And in addition to Gracie, I just gave birth to our son, Deacon James Woodie. He was born December 29, 2004.

I wanted to say thank you for being obedient that day and for being sensitive to the Holy Spirit. I believe that was a turning point in my marriage, faith, and hope. God is faithful to those who trust fully in Him and wait for His timing. He continues to prove it over and over.

God bless you,
JJ and Tracy Woodie

What, you may be wondering, can you do to receive your healing? Based on the gospel's account of this desperate woman, there are a number of things. First, fill your mind with the miracles of Jesus. Read them over and over again until your mind is totally saturated with them. Remember, the thing that birthed faith in the heart of this woman was the things she had heard about Jesus.[17] Romans 10:17 says, "...faith cometh by hearing, and hearing by the word of God" (KJV).

Secondly, get rid of all hurt and bitterness. Nothing poisons our spirit faster than unforgiveness. James 5:16 says, "...confess your sins to each other and pray for each other so that you may be healed." If this woman had held onto her hurt and the injustices she had suffered, she would never have been able to reach out and touch Jesus.

Finally, step out in faith. Risk disappointment. Risk misunderstanding and embarrassment. James 5:14-16 says, "Is any one of you sick? He should call the elders of the church to pray over him and anoint him with oil in the name of the Lord. And the prayer offered in faith will make the sick person well; the Lord will raise him up. If he has sinned, he will be forgiven…The prayer of a righteous man is powerful and effective."

This woman had to fight her way through physical weakness, segregation, and twelve years of negative results, not to mention the press of the crowd, in order to receive her healing. Let her be your example. Get out of your comfort zone. Attend a meeting where they pray for the sick, even if you have never done anything like that before. Act on your faith. Press through your doubts and discouragements. Put past disappointments behind you. Persevere in faith and prayer until you hear Him say, "'Daughter, your faith has healed you. Go in peace and be freed from your suffering.'"[18]

CHAPTER THREE

The
Adulteress

John 8:2-11

CLUTCHING MY CLOTHES ABOUT ME, I stumble barefoot across the temple courts. It is still dark, an hour or two before daylight, and we are alone. Furtively I glance about looking for a way of escape. As if reading my mind, one of the heavy-handed guards tightens his grip on my arm. "Don't try it," he says, "you'll only make things worse."

Another man materializes out of the darkness. "This way," he says, motioning for us to follow him. He takes us to a small room where a single candle flickers on a low table. One of the guards shoves me toward the far corner and tells me to sit. Turning my back to the men I try to arrange my clothes, such as they are. My sandals are missing, as is the covering for my head, and my robe is badly torn.

Sitting on the floor, with my arms wrapped around my knees, I try to reconstruct the events of the last hour. Everything happened so quickly. The door was kicked open and rough hands jerked me to my feet. I grabbed for the sheet, trying to cover my nakedness, as I was pulled from the bed. The man, one of my regulars, dressed quickly. I called to him, but he would not look my way. As he slipped into the night, I saw a third man hand him a money bag.

That I was set up is now obvious, but why? I have always been discreet. Never have I done anything to embarrass a client. Try as I might I cannot think of anyone who would want to destroy me.

Through the wall I hear the murmur of voices, then a rapping on the door. One of the guards releases the latch and several men crowd into the room. For an instant I fear that I am about to be abused, but after a cursory glance my way they ignore me. Though they are speaking in low voices, my ears are sharp and the room is small.

"Well done," says a man I recognize as one of the leading Pharisees. "We will wait until a crowd gathers and then we will confront this Jesus of Nazareth."

He relishes the moment, anyone can see that. With a self-satisfied smirk he adds, "No matter how He responds we will have Him. If He tells us to stone her as the law commands,[19] we will report Him to the Romans.[20] On the other hand, if He tells us to let her go, He will be guilty of breaking the Law of Moses."

I'm not sure who this Jesus is, but it is apparent that I am just a pawn in their game. What happens to me—whether I live or die—is no concern of theirs. For the first time I realize just how perilous my position is. That I will be publicly humiliated is certain, but that seems of little consequence now. If these fanatical Pharisees have their way, I could be stoned!

Frantically my eyes roam the room searching for a way of escape. Although the guards are paying me no mind, escape appears impossible. There is only one door and they have placed themselves squarely in front of it. The only window is small and located high in the wall, well beyond my reach. Disappointed, I bide my time. I will try to make my break when they take me to this Jesus.

The murmur of voices continues but I am no longer listening. Turning to a technique I perfected long ago, I escape to a place deep inside myself. In this inner sanctum, my father is not dead, nor does my mother marry a man who is more interested in me than he is in her. Here my mother cares about me. She does not turn a blind eye to the evil my stepfather has brought into our home. Here my nights are not filled with a fearful dread, nor is my sleep fitful. Here there is no shame, no self-loathing. Here there is....

My escape within is short-lived. A rough hand jerks me to my feet and shoves me toward the door. Stepping into the temple courts, I am momentarily blinded by the brightness of the early morning sun. As my eyes adjust to the light, I see a large group of people clustered together across the way. Apparently that is our destination, for one of the temple guards gives me a shove in that direction. Wildly I look about seeking a way out, but there is none. I am surrounded by a group of Pharisees and some teachers of the Law. In addition, a pair of temple guards are positioned on each side of me, firmly gripping my arms.

Seeing I cannot escape, I muster what dignity I can. Though I am a disheveled mess, I will not grovel before these so-called holy men. Nothing I have ever done in my tragic life can compare with the travesty they have concocted. I may be a woman of the night, but I have never betrayed an innocent or sold my soul to do evil to another. The only person I have ever hurt is myself.

Nearing the edge of the crowd, the chief Pharisee pauses while some of the younger men clear a path. "Make way," they shout, "make way."

Pushing through the throng, he stops directly in front of the Teacher who is sitting on a step. Motioning for the guards to bring me forward he says, "Teacher, this woman was caught in the act of adultery. In the Law, Moses commanded us to stone such women. Now what do You say?"

Glancing around, I see that the crowd is edging closer. There is more than a hint of violence in the air, and I am sure they can feel it. Although the question was intended primarily as a means to trap the Teacher, emotions are running high, and I can't help but think how quickly a crowd can turn into a mob. Looking closer, I am stunned to see that some of the more zealous Pharisees have already armed themselves with stones. The feverish light of fanaticism burns brightly in their eyes.

Towering over Jesus, a smug look of contempt firmly etched on his haughty features, the chief Pharisee wills Him to answer. Without looking up the Teacher stoops down and begins to write on the ground with His finger. Although I cannot read, and thus have no idea what He is writing, I sense that it is troubling to those who have brought this trouble on me. The smirk is gone from the face of the chief Pharisee, who is now red with anger. "Enough of this," he blusters, but the Teacher pays him no mind.

The others push forward, crowding close around us in an effort to read what Jesus is writing. Frightened though I am, I cannot help but marvel at the way He has turned the tables on them, and without uttering a word. In their discomfort, the Pharisees and the teachers of the law are muttering. Now and then one of them will hurl a question at Him, but He doesn't even bother to look up.

In their anger they are growing impatient, and now the questions come hard and fast. "Do we stone her or not?"

"There's no question of her guilt. We caught her in the very act. The Law is clear. What say You?"

"Are You wiser than Moses who gave us the Law of God?"

Finally, Jesus looks up and waits for them to grow silent. "If any one of you is without sin, let him be the first to throw a stone at her." Without waiting for a reply, He stoops down and resumes writing.

I am stunned. With a single sentence, He has turned the tables on them. This is no longer about my sins, but theirs.

For a moment nothing happens, then I sense a movement to my right. Glancing that way I see the chief Pharisee turn to go. His haughty look is gone, replaced by one of chagrin. Behind me I hear the clatter of stones dropping on the pavers in the temple court, then the shuffle of feet. One by one the teachers of the Law and the Pharisees file out.

When they are all gone, Jesus stands up and looks me full in the face. With an effort I force myself to meet His eyes. There is no judgment in them, yet I feel so ashamed. Never have I felt more unworthy, never has my shameful life seemed more unacceptable, yet I have never felt more loved. The way He looks at me makes me know that my life is precious to Him, more precious than it has ever been to me.

"Woman, where are your accusers?" He asks. "Has no one condemned you?"

> The way He looks at me makes me know that my life is precious to Him, more precious than it has ever been to me.

He called me woman—a term of respect in our culture! Why, I cannot remember the last time someone spoke to me with such kindness. He might have called me almost anything else and I would have deserved it, but He did not.

I can hardly speak so great is the lump that has formed in my throat. Finally I manage to say, "No one, Lord. No one."

No one that is except myself. Better than anyone, I know what a sinful life I have lived, how deserving of judgment I am. How pathetic my rationalization now seems, how self-serving. Shame washes over me, and I drop my eyes.

Once again the all-too-familiar voices start their incessant accusations. "You are to blame," they say. "It is your fault. Your stepfather did not come to your bed in the dark hours after midnight because he was evil, but because you were. If he hurt you, shamed you, it must be because you deserved it. Child though you were, the fault lay with you."

Now I hate myself for what I am and for what I have become. I turn to go, to return to the life I have designed as a kind of self-made hell. It is what I deserve, of this I am sure, and if no one else will punish me, I will punish myself.

"Wait," He says, and the kindness in His voice stops me in my tracks. "Neither do I condemn you. Go now and leave your life of sin."

Instantly tears are glistening in my eyes and spilling down my face. He has not excused my sin, nor pretended that it is inconsequential. He has done something far better—He has forgiven me! He has set me free from my shameful past. He has given new life to me.

For the first time, since that long ago night, the accusing voices within are silent. Their debilitating condemnation, their discordant harmony, has been replaced by His song of love. Over and over again I hear Him say, "Neither do I condemn you. Go now and leave your life of sin."

As I slip through the crowd, a new thought takes shape in my mind. At first it is only a faint impression, but as I focus on it, it becomes clear and an amazing thought it is. If He will not condemn me, then who am I to condemn myself? And if He has forgiven me, how dare I not forgive myself?

Life Lessons

LIFE LESSONS

The Adulteress

THERE IS NO QUESTION OF her guilt—this woman was caught in the very act of adultery—still Jesus does not condemn her. Instead, He forgives her and calls her into a new life free from sin.[21] He is "'...the Lamb of God, who takes away the sin of the world!'"[22] and He took her sin away.

I cannot read this account without being overwhelmed by His love and mercy. She was guilty. The Law was clear. She should die. Yet, He does not condemn her. Mercy trumps justice and love conquers all. On that fateful morning, in the midst of a crowd of vipers, she encountered love incarnate and her life was never the same.

Well do I remember the moment it happened for me; the moment when His unconditional love went from a theological concept to a heart reality, from a dusty doctrine to a life-changing experience. I can remember it as clearly as if it happened only yesterday.

It was a Monday morning in the spring of 1973. My pastor, S. Worth Williams, was sitting across the desk from me at Lester Goodson Pontiac in Houston, Texas. Leaning forward he looked at me with intense eyes. Finally he said, "Richard, I want you to think of the worst thing you have ever done."

When I had that dark deed firmly fixed in my mind, I nodded toward him. "Now," he said, "I want you to think of that moment in your life when you were most like Christ, that moment when you were most obedient to the Holy Spirit."

That was more difficult. How quickly we forget those shining moments of Christlikeness, but it seems we can never forget our sinful failures. Finally I thought of something, and I don't mind telling you it seemed rather inconsequential in comparison to my sin.

Numbly I nodded, and then he asked me the question that revolutionized my life. "Richard, when did God love you best; in the moment of your shining Christlikeness or in the moment of your sinful failure?"

Suddenly I had an epiphany, a spiritual experience, a revelation of God's unconditional love. In a voice thick with emotion, I managed to say, "God loves me best always!"

Think about it. If God loves us best always that means there is absolutely nothing we can do to make God love us less. There is no deliberate disobedience, no willful wondering, no shameful failure or degenerate act that will ever make God love us less. Jeremiah says, "The steadfast love of the LORD never ceases, his mercies never come to an end; they are new every morning...."[23]

By the same token, if there is nothing we can do to ever make God love us less, then it must also be true that there is absolutely nothing we can do to make God love us more. No matter how selflessly we live, no matter how faithfully we serve, no matter how much we give, God will never love us more, not even if we were to die a martyr's death. God already loves us totally and completely, as much as He is capable of loving anyone. The proof of His love is Christ on the cross. "But God demonstrates his own love for us in this: While we were still sinners, Christ died for us."[24]

In reality we are the objects of God's love, but we are not the cause of it. He does not love us because we are loveable, for if the truth be known, we are not. Nor does He love us because we so desperately need to be loved, though we do. God loves us because that is the kind of God He is.

"The LORD is compassionate and gracious,

slow to anger, abounding in love…

he does not treat us as our sins deserve

or repay us according to our iniquities.

For as high as the heavens are above the earth,

so great is his love for those who fear him;

as far as the east is from the west,

so far has he removed our transgressions from us…

But from everlasting to everlasting

the LORD's love is with those who fear him…."[25]

If, like this woman caught in the very act of adultery, you are trapped in your sins, I want you to know that Jesus loves you. He loves you just the way you are, but He loves you too much to leave you that way. More than anything, He wants to forgive your sins and set you free—free to be all you were meant to be in Christ.

Don't pretend to be something you are not. Don't try to justify your sinful lifestyle or explain away your guilt. Simply throw yourself on the mercies of God and call on the name of Jesus. First John 1:9 says, "If we confess our sins, he is faithful and just and will forgive us our sins and purify us from all unrighteousness."

CHAPTER FOUR

The Sinner

Luke 7:36-50

IT IS EARLY EVENING AS I hurry toward the home of Simon the Pharisee. Having never ventured into this part of the city, I find that I am more than a little intimidated. Magnificent houses line the quiet streets and I cannot help wondering what it would be like to live in one of them. Just as quickly I dismiss the thought. A woman like me is not welcome here. A fact that is driven home each time I encounter a resident on the street. Most of them act as if I do not exist, but a few have taken pains to display their disdain for me. Although I find their snide remarks painful, it is a small price to pay in order to see Jesus again.

Months have passed since He last visited our city, but not a day has gone by in which He did not inhabit my thoughts. I never tire of talking about Him, and I hungrily devour any news concerning Him. He is revered by the common people, and well He might be considering the miracles He has done, but the religious leaders are becoming more antagonistic every day. I have even heard rumors that they are plotting to kill Him. The very thought makes me nearly mad with fear. I cannot imagine what I would do if something were to happen to Him.

They hate Him, I think, because He is different. They are rigid while He is full of life. He does good at every opportunity while they seem oblivious to human suffering. He cares about people while the only thing they care about is their rules. Once He healed a crippled woman on the Sabbath and they became indignant.[26]

Instead of rejoicing with the woman, one of the synagogue rulers stood up and rebuked her. "There are six days for work. So come and be healed on those days, not on the Sabbath."

Jesus, I was told, just shook His head in amazement. "You hypocrites!" He replied. "You water your ox or your donkey on the Sabbath so why shouldn't this woman, a daughter of Abraham, be set free on the Sabbath day?"

What could they say? They had no answer for Him and the people loved it. They enjoyed seeing the pompous religious leaders taken down a peg or two. Unfortunately, it only seemed to further alienate the Pharisees and the teachers of the Law.

Why then, I find myself wondering, has Simon the Pharisee invited Jesus to dine at his home? Hopefully he has had a change of heart and is now ready to accept Jesus. As much as I want to believe that, I simply cannot. He is an arrogant man and nothing he has ever done leads me to believe he has changed. More likely, he hopes to embarrass Jesus or worse yet, trap Him.

Turning a final corner, I see that a crowd has already gathered at Simon's house. Like me, they have come to be near Jesus, even if they cannot partake of the festivities. Eagerly I scan the open courtyard surrounding the dining area, but I cannot see Jesus. Apparently He has not yet arrived. Turning my attention to the crowd, I wonder how many of them have a story like mine.

Not long ago I was a woman of the night, quite probably the most notorious one in the city. It wasn't a profession I would have chosen, but life conspired to leave me little choice. Although I was good at what I did, I despised myself and with no way out, I lived with a quiet desperation. I hid my hopelessness behind a cynical façade, but on the inside I was dying.

Suddenly a ripple of excitement passes through the crowd, and I push forward to get a better look. Jesus is arriving, and I watch as Simon comes to welcome Him into his home. His greeting is cordial enough, but where are the common courtesies? Simon does not greet Him with a kiss, nor is there water to wash His feet or oil to anoint His head. To ignore these simple courtesies is a deliberate slight, but Jesus refuses to take offense. Around me the crowd is buzzing. Like me, they have seen the Pharisee's none too subtle insult.

Jesus joins Simon and the other guests at the table. It is in the center of the room, surrounded by low couches upon which the guests recline with their heads near the table and their legs extending out. As they eat, I study Jesus. Although He appears at ease, I sense His wariness.

As I observe the guests reclining around the table, I cannot help by notice that Jesus is the only One whose feet have not been washed. It is an insult I cannot ignore and without considering the consequences, I make my way to Him. There is an audible gasp from the onlookers, and Simon glares at me. While it is customary for persons to enter the dining room uninvited, to seat themselves all around against the walls and to converse with those at the table, it is, nevertheless, unheard of for a woman such as me to enter the house of a Pharisee.

Kneeling before Jesus' dusty, sweat-stained feet, I find that I am weeping. No matter what anyone thinks, I am not embarrassed by my actions. To wash His feet with my tears and dry them with my hair seems the least I can do considering what He did for me. Kissing His feet, I hear again the words He first spoke to me so many months ago. "Your sins are forgiven."[27]

His words dispelled the darkness within, washing away all my guilt and fear. There was no shame then, just love and acceptance. For the first time since I was a very small child, I was free from my bitter self-loathing. To wash the feet of the One who cleansed my sin-stained soul seems but a small thing to me. What does it matter what others think?

Fumbling in my garments, I extract a vial of perfume and empty it on His feet. In an instant the room is filled with the fragrance. Shamelessly I loose my hair[28] and wipe His feet with it.

Suddenly a ripple of excitement passes through the crowd, and I push forward to get a better look.

Although I can see nothing but the feet of my Lord, I sense the tension in the room. I have broken propriety. What others think of me is of little concern, but I pray I have not put Jesus in an embarrassing position. Risking a glance at Simon, I see anger has been replaced by a smug self-righteousness. I can read his thoughts as surely as if they were written on his face. *If this man were a prophet, he would know who is touching him and what kind of woman she is—that she is a sinner.* As far as he is concerned, my actions have proven Jesus a fraud.

Before I can do anything Jesus speaks, His clear voice filling this wide room. "Simon, I have something to tell you. Two men owed money to a certain moneylender. One owed him five hundred denarii, and the other fifty. Neither of them had the money to pay him back, so he canceled the debts of both. Now which of them will love him more?"

Sensing a trap, Simon hesitates before finally answering, "I suppose the one who had the bigger debt canceled."

"Well said Simon. You have judged correctly."

Glancing down at me He continues, "Do you see this woman? I came into your house. You did not give me any water for my feet, but she wet my feet with her tears and wiped them with her hair. You did not greet me with a kiss, but this woman, from the time I entered, has not stopped kissing my feet. You did not put oil on my head, but she has poured perfume on my feet. Therefore, I tell you, her many sins have been forgiven—for she loved much."

Risking a look at Simon, I see he has missed the point altogether. Instead of recognizing his own sinfulness, he is glaring at Jesus. Like before, his thoughts are written on his face. *How dare this country bumpkin suggest this sinful woman is more righteous than I? He has insulted me in front of my friends and in my own house at that.*

There is a shadow of sadness on the face of Jesus. Belatedly, I realize that He does not consider Simon an enemy to be destroyed but a wayward friend to be restored. He is looking at him the same way He looked at me when I stood before Him a lost and broken soul. There

There is no condemnation in His eyes, just a wounded love.

is no condemnation in His eyes, just a wounded love. How Simon can resist the appeal of His love is more than I can comprehend.

Tearing his eyes away from Simon, Jesus looks me full in the face. Like the first time, I sense the depth of His passion. His hatred for sin and all the suffering it brings burns like a fire in His eyes, as does His holy love for me. More than anything He wills to undo the damage I have done to myself.

Now His eyes bore into mine. It is as if He can see the struggle I have had these past months. The struggle to believe I have been truly forgiven and more importantly to forgive myself. Now He speaks with an intensity that grips me in the deepest part of my soul. "Your sins are forgiven. Your faith has saved you; go in peace."

There is life in His words and healing too. Inside of me, I feel the bony hand of condemnation lose its grip. The suffocating memories, the black hole of despair, the self-loathing, are all gone. In their place there is light and life. He has made a new woman out of me, and I feel like an innocent.

Turning to Simon and his guests He says, "Her many sins have been forgiven."

I have been publicly exonerated and my heart is singing. A past like mine is nearly impossible to live down, but now that won't be necessary. I am a new woman, and everyone present knows what He has done for me. Overcome with emotion I find myself kissing His feet again. I cannot stop. This itinerant holy man is truly the Son of God. He is my Lord and my Savior!

Life Lessons

The Sinner

WHEN I READ LUKE'S ACCOUNT of this woman's selfless act of love, I see a picture of her in my mind. She is kneeling at the feet of Jesus and her face is transfused with joy. Although she is weeping, there is no sorrow in her tears, only a wordless outpouring of worship. She is literally overwhelmed by what He has done for her, and no expression of her love is too extravagant. Having nothing to give Him but her devotion, she pours out her love in the only way she knows how. She washes His feet with her tears and dries them with her hair.

I once knew a young woman who worshipped with that kind of uninhibited abandonment. She was a member of the church where I was serving as pastor. Her worship was so sincere, so spontaneous, so filled with joy that I sometimes stopped worshipping just to watch her. Over a period of weeks her worship changed. Not all at once but little by little the joy went out of her face. She still worshipped but not with the exuberant enthusiasm that once characterized her praise.

In those days we ended each service with a time of prayer around the altars at the front of the church. As pastor I moved from person to person encouraging them as they prayed. Always when I came to her she was weeping piteously, sorrow leaking from every pore of her being. Something was terribly wrong, anyone could see that, but I had no idea what it might be.

Consequently, I wasn't surprised when she called the office and scheduled an appointment. Taking the chair across from me, she was visibly agitated. With absolutely no preamble she said, "Pastor, I've come to tell you good-bye. I won't be coming to church anymore."

Thinking I might have hurt her feelings I asked, "Have I done something to offend you?"

"No, Pastor."

"Has someone else offended you?"

"No, it's nothing like that."

"If no one has offended you, what is it?"

In a voice thick with emotion, she said, "You don't want to know."

After a moment I replied, "It's not that I want to know, I need to know. If I don't know what it is that's troubling you, how can I help you?"

She sat in painful silence for two or three minutes, twisting a tissue. Finally, she spoke in a voice I had to strain to hear. "Are you sure you want to hear this?"

Kindly as I could I said, "I need to hear it, and you need to tell me."

Taking several deep breaths, she forced herself to look me in the eye. Her words came out in a rush, "I'm having an affair with my boss. He's old enough to be my father. I'm friends with his wife, I baby-sit with his kids, and I hate myself."

Having started she plunged ahead, "You've seen me praying at the end of service. Do you know what I'm doing? I'm begging God to forgive me. I'm promising Him I will never do it again if He will forgive one more time. Yet, even as I'm bargaining with God, another part of my mind is already planning my next clandestine rendezvous."

Stumbling to a stop she struggled to control her emotions. Finally she said, "Pastor, I know I'm a sinner, but

I'm no hypocrite, and I'm not coming back to church until I get my life straightened out."

"You can do that if you want to," I said, "but I pray that you don't. The only hope you have of ever getting your life straightened out is if you stay in church."

In amazement she asked, "Are you telling me, knowing what you know about me, that you still want me to come to church?"

"Absolutely."

"How do you think God feels about it?"

"God is grieved by your sin, but He still loves you as much as He always has. More than anything He wants to forgive your sin and heal your hurts."

"That sounds too good to be true," she mumbled.

"Next time you pray why don't you say something like this: 'Lord, I hate what I'm doing, but I seem powerless to stop. My best intentions are just that—good intentions—nothing more. Even though I know what I am doing is a sin, there is a part of me that cannot get enough. And as hard as it is too believe, there is another part of me that truly loves You and wants to be Yours. Don't give up on me.

If You can keep loving me just a little longer, surely I will become the person You have called me to be.'"

She left without making any promises and the next Sunday she was not in church, nor the Sunday after that. For several weeks she did not darken the church door, and my heart hurt for her. Then one week she returned and sat near the back. She hardly worshipped at all. Her emotions were raw and she wept throughout the service. The following week she returned, and each week thereafter. It was obvious that she was still struggling, but at least she was attending church.

One day several weeks later she burst into my office unannounced. "I've quit my job," she said.

"Do you have a new job?"

"No, but I finally realized that if I ever hope to be free of my sinful relationship with my boss, I had to cut off all contact with him. I decided it was better to be unemployed and in right relationship with Jesus than to have a good job and bust hell wide open."

What good intentions could not do, what shame could not do, what even the fear of eternal damnation could not do, the unconditional love of Jesus did. Through all the weeks and months of her sinful wondering, He refused to abandon her. His love would not let her go, and in the end it was His love that brought her back.

Thinking about her now, these many years later, I'm reminded of Jesus' parable of the lost sheep.

> "'Suppose one of you has a hundred sheep and loses one of them. Does he not leave the ninety-nine in the open country and go after the lost sheep until he finds it? And when he finds it, he joyfully puts it on his shoulders and goes home. Then he calls his friends and neighbors together and says, "Rejoice with me; I have found my lost sheep." I tell you that in the same way there will be more rejoicing in heaven over one sinner who repents than over ninety-nine righteous persons who do not need to repent.'"[29]

When we fall into sin, the enemy of our souls tries to convince us that God is ready to wash His hands of us, but that isn't true. Instead, we become the objects of His special loving attention. Like the good shepherd in this parable, Jesus leaves the ninety-nine and goes into the wasteland of sin in search of us. He doesn't stop searching when it gets dark or when a storm blows up or even when it becomes dangerous or seems hopeless. No! He keeps searching until He finds us.[30]

As James S. Stewart, the great Scottish preacher, often said, "...there is nothing in heaven or earth so dogged and determined and stubborn and persistent as the grace that wills to save!"[31] His love simply will not let us go.

Maybe you've lost your way and made a real mess out of your life. Don't despair, no matter how hopeless your situation seems. God's grace is greater than your sin, and He still believes in you. If He could transform this sinful woman in Luke 7, He can do the same thing for you. If He could restore the fallen woman who became entangled in an adulterous affair with her boss, He can restore you.

Throw yourself on the mercies of God and He will save you. Admit that you are powerless to save yourself or to fix the mess you have made of your life. Ask Jesus to forgive your sins and heal your hurts. Remember, "...if anyone is in Christ, he is a new creation; the old has gone, the new has come! All this is from God, who reconciled us to himself through Christ...."[32]

CHAPTER FIVE

The
Paralytic

John 5:1-15

PUSHING MYSELF A LITTLE HIGHER on my mat, I survey the misery around me. The porch where I have been placed is located in the center of five covered porches surrounding a rather large pool of water. Two pools to be exact, with a dividing wall separating the northern and southern pools. The pools are located near the gate where the sheep enter on their way to the temple to be sacrificed. In Aramaic it is called the pool of Bethesda, meaning "house of mercy."[33] It might more aptly be called a house of misery, for all five porches are littered with a great mass of suffering humanity.[34] We are a disease-ridden lot, blind, lame, and paralyzed. The stench of our sickness is nearly overpowering, matched only by the abject hopelessness that pervades this place.

The newcomers are not hard to spot. Hope still burns in their eyes and they huddle near the edge of the pool, waiting for an angel who never comes. Early on they are attended by family members and compassionate friends, but as the weeks turn into months and the months into years, the caregivers drift away. Having been abandoned by those they love, some of the sick simply give up hope and die.

Why are we brought here? Not to die, I can assure you, but to be healed. It is believed that at certain times an angel stirs up the water. When he does, the first person into the pool is supposed to be healed of whatever disease he has.[35] Maybe it works, I don't know. I've been here thirty-eight years and I've never seen an angel, but I have seen a number of people nearly drown after throwing themselves into the pool. I might have been one of them, but I'm paralyzed from the waist down making me nearly immobile, and I've never had anyone to help me into the water.

Reaching behind me I locate the cloth bag containing my meager rations. The bread is moldy and the cheese old, but I hardly notice. Beggars cannot be choosey, and after all these years I have grown used to it. Indeed, was it not for the charity of a few kind souls many of us would starve to death.

In the early months of my confinement, when hope still burned bright, my family came almost every day bringing fresh fruit and other items. They bathed me and exercised my dead legs, but when it became apparent that I wasn't going to be healed, they came less and less frequently. Then they didn't come at all.

In those days I became an angry man. I found myself enraged with the Almighty. In frustration I called curses down on those who had abandoned me, and I prayed to die. All to no avail. My ranting accomplished nothing and little by little my rage hardened into cynicism. The faith of my youth died. I simply could not serve a God who seemingly turned a blind eye to those who needed Him most.

To my way of thinking, God was to blame for my plight. Could He not have prevented the fall that turned my well-muscled legs into dead sticks? Failing there, could He not have healed me? Did He not hear my mother's desperate prayers? Did her tears mean nothing to Him?

With an effort I redirected my thoughts. After all these years I should know better than to go there. Nothing good can come of rehashing things that cannot be changed. It is simply an exercise in futility.

This being the Sabbath and a feast day,[36] there are more visitors than usual. Most are family members having come from afar to pay a duty visit. They don't stay long; the misery here is too great. Once they have done their duty, they are only too happy to rejoin the throngs who have come to celebrate in the Holy City.

Having nothing better to do, I study those who have come while feigning a bored disinterest. I read their faces like a scholar reviewing a familiar text. Although the expressions vary from person to person, they never really change. I've seen them all—pity, shock, sorrow, disgust. You name it and I've seen it etched on the features of those who have loved ones here. They do not intend to be cruel, probably they are not even aware of their expressions, but they cannot help themselves. The conditions here are simply too tragic, and their response is too visceral to hide.

Out of the corner of my eye I see a handful of men approaching. Although I do not recognize them, they seem to be heading my way. What they could want with me I do not know. Of one thing I am sure, I will not allow them to use me. I am not going to be anyone's good deed. If they need to atone for some misdeed, let them find someone else to be the object of their pity.

Now they are standing directly in front of me. Determining to ignore them I put a scowl on my face.

Although I have not made eye contact or acknowledged their presence in any way, they have not moved. After a bit the man in the forefront squats down forcing me to look Him in the eye. I glare at Him, daring Him to feel sorry for me. He is not intimidated. His gaze does not waver.

I pride myself on reading faces, but His is inscrutable. Finally He speaks. "Do you want to get well?"

What kind of a question is that? Is He mocking me? Does He think I'm paralyzed by choice? Does He think I enjoy walking on my hands while dragging these useless legs?

I want to be angry. I will myself to be sarcastic, but I can't pull it off. For the first time in years, my anger seems contrived. There's no energy there.

Against my will, it seems, I find myself answering respectfully. "Sir, I have no one to help me into the pool when the

I glare at Him, daring Him to feel sorry for me. He is not intimidated. His gaze does not waver.

water is stirred. While I am trying to get in, someone else goes down ahead of me."

Although I have not really answered His question, He seems satisfied. Now He looks at me, willing me to believe. For a moment the world is reduced to the two of us. In my mind there is no past, no misspent youth, no tragic accident, no crippling injury, no thirty-eight years of misery. There is only this moment and the wordless hope it has birthed. As His eyes bore into mine, something of His indomitable will is imparted to me.

Something is happening inside of me, of that I am sure, but just what I do not know. Every fiber of my being is pulsating, even my long dead legs. I want to examine them, but I cannot take my eyes off of His face. There is strength there and compassion. Not pity, but compassion. And from Him I am able to draw strength for myself.

Suddenly His voice rings out like a clap of thunder. "Get up!" He commands. "Pick up your mat and walk."

Instantly I leap to my feet! Although I haven't been able to stand since that fateful night thirty-eight years ago, I now find myself on my feet. Tearing my gaze away from His face, I examine my legs. The dead sticks are gone. My legs are whole, well-muscled, the way I remember them from the days of my youth.

Turning toward Him I take a step in His direction. Holding up a hand He says, "Pick up your mat and walk."

Even though everything within me yearns to go to Him, I do as He bids. Rolling up my mat, I cannot help but notice the excitement that has swept through this suffering mass. Everyone is talking at once and those who are able are crowding close, trying to touch me.

Once more I turn toward Him, only to discover that He is gone. Anxiously I search the crowd, but He is nowhere to be seen. Momentarily I am disappointed. I don't even know His name. How will I ever thank Him?

Placing my worn mat on my shoulder, I look around one last time. For thirty-eight years, this place of misery has been my home. My family literally carried me here, hoping for a miracle. When it became apparent one was not forthcoming, they abandoned me to my fate—a fate worse than death. But He had other plans, this Miracle Worker.

Now I cannot get out of here fast enough. Pushing my way through the suffering mass, I make my way into the street where I look around in amazement. Things look so different. I hardly recognize anything. Involuntarily my gaze is drawn toward the temple towers which gleam against the bright blue of the sky. I cannot remember the last time I was there, and now I find that I am yearning for the courts of the Lord. If I cannot thank the One who healed me, at least I can give God praise.

I have only gone a short distance when I am accosted by a group of "pious" Jews. In an instant they are in my face, wagging their fingers accusingly. "What do you think you are doing?" they demand. "It is the Sabbath; the Law forbids you to carry your mat."

Now I remember why I wearied of religion. It is so grim, so joyless, nothing more than an impossibly long list of rules. Ducking my shoulder I try to force my way past them, but it is no use.

Putting my mat down I face them, anger coloring my words. "Do you know who I am? Do any of you recognize me?"

"I thought not. Thirty-eight years ago I was in a terrible accident that left me paralyzed from the waist down. All those years I lay by the pool of Bethesda waiting for someone to help me into the water, but no one came. No one."

"Enough of this," one of them interrupts. "What does that have to do with carrying your bed on the Sabbath?"

"I'm coming to that. The Man who made me well said to me, 'Pick up your mat and walk.'"

"Who is this fellow? Tell us His name and we will deal with Him."

"I don't know who He is. I never saw Him before today. When I tried to thank Him, He had disappeared into the crowd."

I leave them arguing among themselves and make my way into the temple. Try as I might I cannot recapture my earlier joy. Though my body is whole, I am still eaten up with bitterness. In my mind I find myself lashing out at the do-gooders. If that is what God is like, I want nothing to do with Him.

I am still fuming when I suddenly find myself face-to-face with the Healer. Before I can say anything He says, "See, you are well again. Stop sinning or something worse may happen to you."

His words take me back and in an instant, I am reliving my misspent youth. Guilt washes over me and shame. Then anger. How dare He suggest I got what was coming to me. I was no different from a hundred other young men, a thousand.

Now I am really mad. Who does He think He is telling me to stop sinning or something worse may happen? Is He trying to scare me?

Grabbing a bystander I demanded, "Who was that man? The One who was talking to me."

"That's the Prophet," he said. "Jesus of Nazareth."

Retracing my steps I find the Jews just where I left them, still embroiled in a heated argument. Shouldering my way into their midst I shout until I have their attention. "The man who healed me, the One who told me to carry my bed on the Sabbath, I know who He is."

I pause for a moment while they press around me. Then I say, "His name is Jesus. Jesus of Nazareth."

I linger just long enough to see that my words have had the desired effect, and then I fade into the crowd. As I am leaving I hear them discussing the Healer's fate. "At last we have grounds to accuse Him. He has broken the Sabbath and commanded this man to do so as well. He will not get away with this."[37]

Momentarily I regret my hasty actions, but with an effort I push my guilt aside. His fate is no concern of mine. I don't owe Him anything, even if He did heal me. Besides, He should have shown me more respect.

As I wander through the narrow streets, reacquainting myself with the Holy City, I realize that in spite of my healing I am still a bitter man. My crippled legs are whole, but my heart is sick. I view everyone with a jaundice eye.

For just a moment, I wonder if the Healer could do anything about this sickness in my soul. Just as quickly I dismiss the thought. Even if He could change my heart, I would not allow it. There are some wounds I will never forgive, some hurts I will never let go. I have learned my lesson. Love and trust just make it possible for others to betray you. My cynicism is my strength. No one is going to make a fool out of me. Not now. Not ever.

Life Lessons

LIFE LESSONS

The Paralytic

LIKE MANY OF THE PEOPLE who received a miracle at the hands of Jesus, this man remains a mystery. We know almost nothing about him. We do not know his name or anything about his family or where he came from. John tells us only that he was "an invalid for thirty-eight years."[38]

Although we do not know what caused his condition, the Scriptures seem to suggest that personal sin plagued his life. I mention this because Jesus went to great length on other occasions to disassociate an individual's illness from their personal sin or the sins of their parents.[39] However, on this occasion, and uncharacteristically, He makes it a point to tell this man, "Stop sinning or something worse may happen to you."[40]

I am not suggesting that his condition was God's way of punishing him for his sins. If that were the case, we would all be sick, for who among us has not sinned? As a young man he probably made some sinful and irresponsible decision that resulted in a tragic accident that left him crippled.

Now that he has been restored to health, Jesus tells him to change his ways or something worse might happen.

In many ways he seems an unlikely candidate for a healing. Apparently he knew nothing about Jesus or the miracles He had done. If he was hoping or praying that Jesus would heal him, the Scriptures make no mention of it. Nor is there anything said about his faith. For reasons known only to God, Jesus chose to heal him without any effort on his part.

Perhaps he received his healing precisely because he was such an unlikely candidate. By healing him Jesus demonstrates that none of us need despair, regardless of how lacking our faith may be. Nor should we give up no matter how long we have suffered or how desperate our situation seems to be.

We see this same principle at work in the conversion of Saul.[41] He was not seeking Jesus. In fact, he was on a mission to persecute the followers of Christ when the Lord saved him. Later, he would reason that the very fact that Jesus saved him—the greatest of all sinners—was proof that no one is so lost that he cannot be found.[42] He writes, "But God had mercy on me so that Christ Jesus could use me as an example to show everyone how patient he is with even the worst sinners, so that others will realize that they, too, can have everlasting life."[43]

Could it be that Jesus is using the healing of this paralytic in much the same way? Is it an example for us, an object lesson? If Jesus was willing to go out of His way to heal this undeserving man, a man whose condition likely resulted from his own sinful and irresponsible behavior, then surely there is no one beyond the reach of His compassion. Does not this healing demonstrate that no matter what you may have done to cause your illness, Jesus still cares for you? He is touched by the things you suffer, even those you bring on yourself.[44]

Finally, let me point out that although this man received a physical healing, it appears his heart was unchanged. He was only too willing to obey Jesus when it came to his physical healing,[45] but when Jesus tried to address his spiritual needs, he resented it.[46] John tells us that he immediately went out and told the Jews it was Jesus who had healed him.[47] "So, because Jesus was doing these things on the Sabbath, the Jews persecuted him."[48]

Normally when I read of the miracles of Jesus my heart leaps within me, but when I finished this account, I was grieved in my spirit. I was reminded again of how often we seek the Lord's blessing without allowing Him to change our hearts. A physical healing is a wonderful thing, but it pales in comparison to the greatest miracle of all—the transformation of our hearts. How tragic to encounter the Savior without allowing Him to deliver us from our sinful self.

As you consider these things, let me encourage you to examine your own life. Do you need a physical healing? Does someone you love need one? If so, let this account encourage you. Even if you have little or no faith, you need not despair. Even if you feel you are to blame for your condition, you need not lose hope. Even if you have been sick for a long time, there is no reason to give up.

Hebrews 4:16 exhorts us to "approach the throne of grace with confidence, so that we may receive mercy and find grace to help us in our time of need."

Our confidence is not based on our personal goodness or merit, but on the character of God. We do not focus on ourselves or even our need, but on His sufficiency. We remind ourselves that if He healed a man like this paralytic, then surely He will intervene on our behalf. More importantly we remember Romans 8:32. "He who did not spare his own Son, but gave him up for us all—how will he not also, along with him, graciously give us all things?" *The*

Message puts it like this, "Is there anything else he wouldn't gladly and freely do for us?"

> "Thou art coming to a king
> Large petitions with thee bring,
> For His wealth and power are such
> That thou canst never ask too much."[49]

"Now to him who is able to do immeasurably more than all we ask or imagine, according to his power that is at work within us, to him be glory in the church and in Christ Jesus throughout all generations, for ever and ever! Amen."[50]

CHAPTER SIX

The Woman at the Well

John 4:1-29

THE SUN IS HIGH IN the sky as I step into the street, causing me to blink as my eyes adjust to the brightness. Placing my water jug on my head, I hurry toward Jacob's well at the far edge of our small village. Although the noonday heat is merciless, I prefer it to the scalding tongues of the village wags, who gather at the well in the cool of the evening.

I walk swiftly, with a purpose, looking neither to the left nor the right. Both my posture and my stride are designed to discourage interruption should I meet anyone. It's not that I am antisocial, although it may appear that way. If the truth be known, I crave relationships and this craving has been my undoing. More often than not I am too gullible, too naive, too easily taken in, especially when it comes to men.

Why am I so needy? Who knows, maybe I was born this way. Or maybe I grew up with a hole in my soul, a hole created by my relationship with my father, or lack thereof.

Maybe if my father had been more attentive, more affectionate, I would not have this inordinate need for masculine attention.

Rounding a final corner I am startled to see a stranger sitting near the well. He is a Jew from the looks of Him and a tired one at that. As I draw near, He offers me a weary smile.

"Would you be kind enough to give Me a drink of water?"

Although He looks Jewish, He must not be, for no self-respecting Jew would speak to a Samaritan, let alone a Samaritan woman. Without really intending to, I find myself putting my thoughts into words. "How can You ask me for a drink since Jews do not associate with Samaritans?"

"If you knew Me—who I am and why I have come—you would ask Me for a drink and I would give you living water."

"How can You do that? The well is deep and You have nothing to draw with."

Gesturing toward the well He says, "Whoever drinks this water will get thirsty again, but whoever drinks the water I give him will never thirst again. The living water I give him will quench the thirst of his soul and give him eternal life."

What an amazing thought—to never thirst again, to never have to draw water or lug this heavy water pot. And if I never had to come to the well, I would not have to risk the demeaning glances or the none too subtle insults of those women who think they are better than me. As I ponder His words and their ramifications, hope leaps in my heart.

"Sir," I cry, "give me this living water so I won't get thirsty and have to keep coming here to draw water."

"Go get your husband and come back."

His command seems innocent enough, but who can know? Already my mind is racing, searching my memories for some recollection of Him. What does He know about me? Is He trying to embarrass me or to make a fool out of me?

This is what I hate about relationships—they are so intrusive. One minute you are having an innocent conversation and the next He is prying into your past, trying to dig up things better left alone. Well, I'm not about to get into that and if He thinks I am, He has another thing coming!

Putting on my most sincere face I reply, "I'm sorry, but I have no husband."

"You are right," He says, looking me in the eye. "The truth is, you have had five husbands, and the man you are living with is not your husband."

Although He has spoken kindly and with great compassion, His words have laid bare my shameful past. A wave of painful memories threatens to engulf me, and I turn away lest He see the tears glistening in my eyes. Taking a deep breath, I compose myself, pushing the memories back beneath the surface of my mind.

"Sir," I say, feigning enthusiasm, "I can see that You are a Prophet. Let me ask You a question that has been troubling me for some time. Our fathers worshipped on this mountain, but according to the Jews, we should be worshipping in Jerusalem. Who's right?"

"My dear woman, the place where you worship is not nearly as important as who you worship and how you worship. God is spirit, and His worshipers must worship Him in spirit and in truth. True worshipers will worship the Father not in form only, but from their heart and in absolute truthfulness. They will not pretend to be something they are not."

Once more He has nailed me. Not unkindly, but with unerring accuracy, for that is what I have been doing all my life—pretending to be something I am not. What I am has never seemed to be good enough, not for my father who wanted a son, nor for my husbands who always found me lacking, and certainly not good enough for God.

Having finally faced this tragic truth, I find myself reliving a host of painful memories. In the first I am a young girl possessed of an agile and inquisitive mind. Although I dutifully performed my domestic duties, I found women's work mindless. I wanted to study the Torah, as my father did, so I taught myself to read, howbeit secretly. Naively, I believed I could win my father's approval by proving I was as smart as any boy.

My opportunity came one day when the rabbi and my father were discussing one of the finer points of the Law. When there was a pause in their discussion I ventured an opinion. My thesis was well thought out, and I articulated it artfully. To my chagrin, both my father and the rabbi were aghast. Angrily my father ordered me out of the room. After I left the rabbi rebuked him, telling him that if any man gave his daughter a knowledge of the Law, it was as though he taught her lechery.[51]

With an effort I push that painful memory from my mind and return to the present. When I do, I find that the Prophet is looking at me with such compassion that I experience a nearly overwhelming urge to bare my soul to Him. As if reading my mind He says, "I know about your relationship with your father and your dreams of being a scholar. I also know about your five marriages. More importantly, I know about your spiritual emptiness and the hunger you can't satisfy."

Rather than being offended at His words, I am fascinated. Without really intending to, I find myself telling Him things I have never told anyone, hesitantly at first, then with a rush of words.

"Shortly after I embarrassed my father in front of the rabbi, he arranged for me to marry a young man who was dull and lacking in ambition. To my father's way of thinking, marriage and babies would put me in my place.

"Although I tried to be a dutiful wife, I think I realized our marriage was doomed from the beginning. My husband was inept at everything and I could not respect a man so lacking, let alone love him. I tried to instruct him, but he found my efforts insulting. When I could not give him children, he turned churlish and mean. I was shamed when he divorced me, but relieved too, for I could not imagine spending the rest of my life in such a loveless marriage.

"Of course my father blamed me for the divorce. To his way of thinking, I was far too headstrong and outspoken. He repeatedly told me that no man wanted a wife who spoke her mind or appeared to be smarter than he was."

While I have been speaking, I have deliberately avoided looking at the Prophet. Now I force myself to look Him full in the face. There is no judgment there, just understanding and something else I can't put my finger on. Relieved, I continue.

"My second husband was an older man whose first wife had died. He was looking for a wife who would care for his children and keep his house. In retrospect, I realize that, like my first marriage, this one was destined to fail. I was hardly older than his children and they resented me from the start. To make matters worse, he was nearly as old as my father, and I could not conceive of being a wife to him. As You might imagine, he also divorced me and in short order.

"There followed two more failed marriages in rapid fashion. I cannot remember the painful details, maybe I don't want to. All that remains is a sense of failure and an ever deepening shame."

I am weeping now, silently. The sorrow I have kept under such tight wrap all these years is now oozing out of me and with it the old hurts I have so carefully kept. Although I am embarrassed by my uncharacteristic emotional display, I feel such relief that I forge ahead.

"Following my fourth divorce, my father washed his hands of me. As far as he was concerned, I was a lost cause and a source of embarrassment to him. Although my mother was sympathetic, she dared not go against my father.

"Being damaged goods, no self-respecting Jewish man would marry me. I considered selling myself into slavery in order to survive, but I couldn't imagine being indentured for life. Instead, I became what is referred to in polite company as a 'woman of the night.' I found it hardly more demeaning than being a wife to a man who considered me his property."

When I find the courage to look up, the Prophet is studying my face with genuine interest. I, in turn, study His. I am looking for any hint of judgment, ready to flee should I find even the slightest suggestion of disapproval.

Try as I might all I can see is a face full of mercy. Taking a deep breath, I resume my confession.

"That's how I met the man who became my fifth and final husband. He was a merchant from Samaria and one of my regulars. My family would have considered him a dog, especially my father. Maybe that's why I found him so attractive, at least at first."

I pause, considering what I have just said. After a moment I simply shake my head. "Talking about it now I can see how pathetic I was, or maybe I should say am. After all those years, I was still allowing my father to control me. Having finally realized I could never win his approval, I was now looking for ways to spite him.

"Be that as it may, I found my Samaritan fascinating. Whereas other men found my wit and intelligence intimidating, he reveled in them. He told me about his business and sought my

When I find the courage to look up, the Prophet is studying my face with genuine interest.

advice. In his eyes I was his equal, and no man had ever treated me like that.

"After two years we were married and he brought me here. I feared for his reputation, but he just laughed it off. And my fears proved groundless, at least as long as he was alive. But once he died the rumors started. Once more I was an outcast, the money he left me not withstanding."

Talking about him has unleashed a fresh wave of grief and I find myself weeping. Although the pain is poignant, there is something different about my grief this time. Always before it has been richly seasoned with anger— anger at God, anger at life's unfairness, anger at my family, anger at the self-righteous townspeople; but this time I am not angry, just sad, terribly sad.

Sad that death has taken the one man who understood me and loved me for the person I am. Sad that I had to mess things up so badly before I found him, and sad that I seem to have reverted to my self-destructive habits now that he is gone. Sad that I made so many poor decisions and spent so much of my life trying to undo the mess I had made. And I am sad that it took me so long to see that I am my own worst enemy.

In my melancholy mood, I find that I am thinking about the Messiah. Turning to the Prophet I say, "When the Messiah comes, He will surely explain everything. Maybe then my life will make some sense. Maybe then I will be the person I have always wanted to be."

Looking at me intently He says, "I am He. The One who speaks to you is the Messiah."

For a moment I am stunned. Could it be? Is it possible that I have been conversing with the Messiah?

He's not at all like what I had been led to expect. The Messiah is supposed to be a mighty warrior, a conquering King, defeating the enemies of Israel. But this Man is no warrior, not by a long shot, nor a conquering King. Yet He has routed the enemies that have held me hostage my whole life long. What no army could ever do, He has done. Using nothing but love

Is it possible that I have been conversing with the Messiah?

and mercy, He has vanquished the inner enemies of shame and self-loathing.

How did this happen? What brought about this incredible liberation? He did, but I cannot explain how He did it.

To my amazement, I feel like an innocent. How can this be? I know too much, I have experienced too much, to ever be a child again. Yet, more than anything else that is the way I feel—like a child running barefoot in the spring or seeing the world for the first time. I feel as if I have stepped into a new life, as if I am a new person. If it wasn't so utterly impossible, I would think I had been born again.

I am nearly mad with wonder, giddy with joy, and He just sits on the well curb smiling, pleasure washing some of the tiredness out of His eyes. How can He be so calm when I am bursting with joy? I want to run and leap, sing and dance, kiss babies and hug strangers. Why, I almost feel tender toward my father. Now that's really something!

Leaving my water jug, I hurry through the streets toward the market. If I don't tell someone what has happened to me, I think I will burst.

As usual, a group of my late husband's friends have congregated in the shadows in the corner of the marketplace to escape the heat. Abandoning all decorum I push my way into their midst, talking excitedly.

"He's here. The Messiah is here! You have to come see Him for yourselves."

"What are you talking about?"

"He knew all about me, even my darkest secrets, and yet He did not reject me. For the first time in my life, I don't have to live a lie. I don't have to pretend to be something I'm not. He loves me just the way I am, and yet His love has made me different somehow, better.

"I am free! I am free, I tell you. Free at last to be the woman I was meant to be.

"Hurry! Come see this Man who told me everything I ever did. He has to be the Messiah. No one else could do that."

Life Lessons

LIFE LESSONS

The Woman at the Well

LIKE MANY OF THE PEOPLE Jesus ministered to, this woman remains anonymous. And like many of the others, she has nothing to recommend her to Jesus except her desperate need. Unlike the others, however, she did not seek Jesus. Instead, He came looking for her. He came to this small village in Samaria for the express purpose of ministering to her—a dysfunctional woman.

Like many of us, she is a person with a flawed past. She has secret sins and hidden failures, things in her past she doesn't want anyone to know. And, like us, she soon learns that, while she may deny them, she cannot escape them. Their persistent painfulness is always just below the surface, and it only takes a knowing glance, or a telling word, to bring it all back.

In her tragic history, we can see much of our own. Not necessarily the marital failure and immorality, but the duplicity and self-deception. She is ashamed of her past, she wishes she could go back and change it, but she can't. Instead, she practices a determined denial. If she doesn't think about it, if she pretends it didn't happen, then perhaps she can escape its painfulness. Unfortunately, that which we deny or repress is held back from His healing grace, and thus lives on to torment us and undermine our most important relationships.

Denial is never an effective way of dealing with sin and failure. If it worked she would have been free of her disastrous past; instead, she is condemned to live under its ever-present shadow. Every time she establishes a new relationship, one in which her past is not known, she lives in constant fear of being found out. Consequently, she is always working on her image, always trying to convince others that she really is the person they perceive her to be.

It isn't hard to imagine her inner turmoil. She wants to be different but doubts that she ever will be. She longs for meaningful friendships but is afraid to let anyone know her. She is convinced that if they knew her as she really is, they would reject her. Yet she experiences no little frustration, for relationships built on falsehood are exhausting and unfulfilling.

Is there any hope for her, for us? Yes, but only if we can "come clean" with ourselves and with God!

Her salvation is in letting Jesus confront her with the truth about her past. That's what He did when she told Him that she had no husband. Instead of letting her off the hook, He confronted her. "You are right when you say you have no husband. The fact is, you have had five husbands, and the man you now have is not your husband...."[52]

That Jesus knew so much about her must have been both terrifying and liberating. Terrifying, because knowing what He does, He might condemn her or worse yet, reject her. It was liberating because she was finally free from the burden of pretending, free from the fear of being found out. Since Jesus already knew the worst about her, she no longer had to pretend to be something she was not. In short order, her shame gave way to joyous wonder for Jesus did not condemn her, nor did He reject her. Instead, He healed and forgave her!

For the first time in years she was at peace. Her inner enemies had been defeated, the accusing voices strangely stilled. In their place was a quiet assurance. She was loved. She was accepted. The past could no longer torment her, for she was forgiven. It could not blackmail her, for it had already been exposed to the light of His loving acceptance.

And here's the good news: What Jesus did for her, He will do for you!

For instance, I recently had the opportunity to minister God's healing grace to a lady who was struggling with the aftermath of incest. Although the tragic incident had occurred more than thirty years earlier, the memories still plagued her. As I stepped to the pulpit that evening to begin my message, the Spirit gave me an inner vision. Suddenly, like slides projected on the screen of my mind, I saw a series of pictures.

In the first picture, I saw a stylishly dressed woman who appeared to be in her forties. On the outside she seemed calm and collected, but on the inside she was tormented. In the second picture, I saw a young girl, of six or seven, run out the screen door of a sagging frame house and onto a wooden porch. She was crying as she stumbled down the steps and ran into the wooded pasture. In the third picture, I saw Jesus take her into His arms. He wiped away her tears and comforted her. Soon she was at peace.

Almost instantly I understood what those pictures meant. After describing them to the congregation, I told them that I believed there was a woman present who had been sexually molested by her uncle when she was seven years old, and that Jesus was present in a special way to heal her. Finally, I prayed a simple healing prayer and the service continued.

After the benediction, an attractive middle-aged woman made it a point to thank me for my ministry. When she did, she handed me a note in which she had written, "I was that seven-year-old girl. My father's cousin molested me and I ran from the house just as you described, and I have been running ever since. I've never told anyone what happened to me, though that experience has haunted me all these years. Tonight Jesus healed me. I feel like a new person."

What He did for her, He will do for you. If you have been victimized by life or loved ones, He comes to heal and restore. If you are living with secret sins and the accompanying fear and guilt, He comes to forgive you. "Therefore, if anyone is in Christ, he is a new creation; the old has gone, the new has come!"[53]

CHAPTER SEVEN

The Syrophenician Woman

Matthew 15:21-28

THE HOUSE IS QUIET AT last but still I pace the floor, my frayed nerves as taunt as a bow string. This last episode was the worst yet, and no matter what I do I can't get the tragic images out of my mind. I'm haunted by the fear and madness in my daughter's eyes. The grotesque contortions into which she twists her face, the guttural male voice spewing obscenities, the self-inflicted wounds, the tearing out of her hair, all mock my motherhood. Worst of all is my helplessness. Try as I might I cannot help her.

A soft moan seeps out of the other room and I move to the doorway and look in, being careful not to wake her. What I see hurts me in a way I cannot put into words. Her limp hair lies on the mat in a tangled mess, her bruised features white and pasty. A patchwork of scars leaves an ugly trail down her thin arms and even in sleep she is tormented.

What, I wonder for the thousandth time, *happened to my beautiful little girl? How did this evil invade our home and* take up habitation in my daughter? Who opened the door to this foul spirit? Was it something I did? Or something her father did?

Never have I felt more helpless. Although I love my daughter more than life itself, I am powerless to help her. Nor have the priests of Astarte—the moon goddess whom we worship—fared any better. Neither their potions nor their incantations have had any effect against the evil spirit that torments her.

Exhausted and overwrought, I turn from the doorway and make my way to a cushion where I collapse in a heap. Though it is mid-afternoon, the room is dark for I have not opened the door or the shutters that cover the window. What my daughter suffers is our private hell, and I will not allow it to become fodder for neighborhood gossip if I can help it.

Wrapping my arms around my pulled up knees, I yield to my grief. Soundless sobs shake my hunched shoulders as I contemplate the bleak future. How long can we live like this, I wonder. Already my husband is finding more and more reasons not to come home, and I am at my wit's end. Depression dogs my days, and I do not know how much longer I can cope.

My melancholy musing is interrupted by someone pounding on the door. For a moment I consider ignoring it, but then I think better of it, lest the noise awaken my daughter. Lunging to my feet, I use the hem of my skirt to wipe my tearstained face.

"Just a moment, I'm coming," I call out, as I hurry toward the door.

Opening the door I find myself face-to-face with my dearest friend. Without giving me a chance to greet her, she bursts out, "He's here. He's right here in our village!"

"What are you talking about?" I ask, as she pushes past me into the house.

Moving to the window she opens the shutters before turning to face me. "The Miracle Worker I told you about. The One I saw in Galilee. Remember I told you how He healed the mute and the blind? More importantly the evil spirits obeyed Him."[54]

Taking my hands in hers, she continues, "This is your chance. He can save your daughter from the evil spirit that is tormenting her!"

I want to believe, I truly do, but there is so much I don't understand. Sensing my hesitation she releases my hands, and I walk to the window and stare down the narrow street. Without looking at her I ask, "Didn't you tell me He was a Jewish prophet, their long awaited Messiah or something like that?"

"So," she says, her tone questioning.

Turning to face her I ask, "What makes you think He will help my daughter? Everyone knows how the Jews feel about Syrophenicians. As far as they are concerned, we are all unclean."

Exasperated she demands, "What do you have to lose?"

A good point and in spite of myself, I find a desperate hope taking hold of my heart. Sensing my interest she presses the issue. "You may never get another opportunity like this. As far as anyone knows, this is the only time Jesus has ever ventured outside the borders of His own country. Perhaps the gods brought Him here just to deliver your daughter."

The same thought had occurred to me and for a moment I allow myself to consider that possibility. "What about my daughter?" I ask. "I can't leave her alone."

"I'll stay with her."

"She's sleeping now, but she could wake up anytime. Who knows what will happen when she does."

"I'll be fine. Just get going."

"What if she becomes violent or worse yet tries to harm herself?"

"I can handle her. Just go."

"Where can I find this Jesus?"

"I saw Him enter a merchant's house near the market, the one with a walled courtyard. You know the one I'm talking about, don't you?"

I nod and before I can change my mind, she hurries me out the door. As I make my way through the narrow streets toward the market, I try to think of the proper way to approach Him. Having had no experience with miracle workers, Jewish or otherwise, I don't know what's expected of me.

Arriving at the merchant's house, I pause to catch my breath. Desperation gives me the courage to open the gate and step into the courtyard. I see a group of men reclining near a table, and they turn

I want to believe, I truly do, but there is so much I don't understand.

to stare at me as I make my way toward them. After a moment they glance at the One I assume must be Jesus to gauge His reaction. He studies my face briefly, then looks away as if to dismiss me.

I, in turn, study Him. He is smaller than I imagined and rather nondescript. His face is deeply lined and weariness clings to Him like fine dust. Exhausted though He obviously is, there emanates from Him an air of authority unlike anything I have ever experienced. Standing in His presence, I feel my hopes rising. *He can deliver my daughter,* I tell myself, *I'm sure of it.*

Although He has done nothing to encourage me, I rush toward Him and fall at His feet. Kneeling there I flash back to the terror of last night. Once more I see my young daughter clawing at her face and hissing like a snake. I try to restrain her, but her strength is tenfold and she hurls me across the room. She glares at me and then laughs hysterically. "She is mine now," growls a menacing voice, emanating from her lips.

Desperately I cry out, "Son of David, have mercy upon me for my daughter is grievously tormented by an evil spirit."

To my consternation He acts as if He has not heard me, as if I haven't uttered a word. "Lord, Son of David," I plead even more urgently, "please don't turn a deaf ear to my cry. If you won't help me for my sake, do it for my daughter. This evil spirit is killing her."

I am sobbing now, begging for His help, but He continues to act as if I am not even there. Finally, His disciples urge Him to do something. "Give her what she wants so she will go away. All this wailing is driving us mad."

Pressing my forehead to the ground at His feet, I plead with Him. "Lord, help me!"

Challenging her faith, He says, "It is not right to take the children's bread and give it to dogs."

Love and desperation combine to give me a boldness I do not normally possess. Lifting my face from the ground, I look

There emanates from Him an air of authority unlike anything I have ever experienced. Standing in His presence, I feel my hopes rising.

Him in the eye, not caring that my tears have mingled with the dust to muddy my cheeks. "That is true," I say, "but even the dogs eat the crumbs that fall from their masters' table."

For a moment I fear that I may have been too brash, but then a glow of pleasure lights His tired face. "Woman, how can I refuse you? Your faith is something else! Go home now; the demon has left your daughter never to return."

I mumble my gratitude while backing toward the gate. Turning, I rush into the street and hurry toward home. Nearing the door I find myself slowing down. I am almost afraid to go in. What if nothing has happened? What if my precious daughter is still in the grip of that malevolent spirit?

With an effort I push those tormenting thoughts from my mind and concentrate on His words, "Go home now; the demon has left your daughter never to return."

Stepping through the door, I immediately sense the difference. The evil presence is gone, and the room is filled with peace. I hurry toward the back of the house where I left my daughter. When she sees me, she squeals with delight and stretches her arms toward me. Rushing to her bed, I scoop her up and crush her against my breast.

"Thank God you are all right," I say over and over again while covering her face with kisses.

Over her shoulder I smile a thank you to my friend who says, "I told you that demon was no match for the Miracle Worker from Galilee."

Life Lessons

LIFE LESSONS

The Syrophenician Woman

I CANNOT HELP COMPARING THIS story with the account of Jairus and his daughter. In both instances a desperate parent seeks the help of Jesus on behalf of their child. This, however, is where the similarities end. Jairus was an influential man, the ruler of the synagogue in Capernaum. This mother was a nameless pagan, a Gentile, a worshipper of the moon goddess Astarte. Jairus's daughter was sick unto death; in fact, she had died. The Syrophenician woman's daughter was demon-possessed. Yet, in each instance Jesus intervened. He restored Jairus's daughter to life and health, and He cast out the demon that was tormenting the Syrophenician woman's daughter.

What can we learn from these two accounts?

1. Jesus is no respecter of persons.

He helped this anonymous Gentile woman just as He helped the influential Jairus. In fact, most of the recipients of His miracles were nameless "nobodies." This should be an encouragement to all of us who have nothing but our neediness to recommend us to Jesus. Our confidence should always rest on His character not our merit. Remember, He does not intervene on our behalf because we are good but because He is.

2. These accounts demonstrate Jesus' power over disease, demons, and death.

By healing the sick, casting out demons, and raising the dead, Jesus demonstrated that with God nothing is impossible.[55] The cruelest diseases, the most debilitating illnesses, were powerless before His healing touch. Luke writes, "...the people brought to Jesus all who had various kinds of sickness, and laying his hands on each one, he healed them."[56]

Nor could demons resist His authority. Mark declares, "For with authority He commands even the unclean spirits, and they obey Him."[57] On at least three occasions, Jesus demonstrated His authority over death by restoring the dead to life—a widow's son,[58] Jairus's daughter,[59] and Lazarus who had been dead four days.[60] Of course, His ultimate triumph over death was His own resurrection.[61]

3. Nothing impresses God more than our faith.

At first Jesus seemed immune to the plight of the Syrophenician woman's daughter. Although this mother pled with Him, He simply ignored her. He did not so much as grace her pleas with a reply. Finally, when she would not be put off, He said, "It is not right to take the children's bread and toss it to their dogs."[62]

Refusing to take offense, she replied, "Yes, Lord, but even the dogs eat the crumbs that fall from their masters' table."[63]

Allow me to paraphrase her words: "Lord, I know Your first responsibility is to the House of Israel, so go ahead and minister to them. Open every blind eye, loose every dumb tongue, unstop every deaf ear, cleanse every leper, and heal every cripple. Cast out every unclean spirit, deliver every demon-possessed person, and even raise the dead. Just let me tag along behind You and pick up the crumbs. That will be more than enough to deliver my daughter."

When she approached Jesus on the basis of her need, He seemed unmoved by her plight. But when she spoke to Him out of her faith, He responded, "Woman, you have great faith! Your request is granted."[64]

Remember, "without faith it is impossible to please God, because anyone who comes to him must believe that he exists and that he rewards those who earnestly seek him."[65]

4. Never underestimate the power of a parent's love or the extremes to which it will go.

A parent's love will keep them pressing for a miracle long past the point of exhaustion. They will deprive themselves of the necessities of life if necessary in order to provide for their child. They will risk ridicule and humiliation, even persecution and death on behalf of their child. A parent's love will prevail when all else fails.

Late one afternoon the telephone rang in the church office. The caller was a member of our congregation, a distraught father seeking my help. I listened as he told me that they had just returned from a consultation with their six-year-old son's doctor. To their dismay, the doctor had informed them that the cancer afflicting Shane had spread from the tumor in his cheek to his kidneys. Shane was in great pain, and he was asking for me. Hesitantly, Rick asked if I could come to their home and pray for him.

Of course my heart went out to them, but I had a scheduling conflict. I was supposed to conduct a wedding rehearsal in forty-five minutes, making it impossible for me to drive across town and return without being late for the rehearsal. I explained my situation and offered two possible solutions. I could drive to their home as soon as the rehearsal was finished, or they could come to the office now. After conferring with his wife, Rick informed me that they were on their way.

When they arrived I brought them into my office. Shane immediately climbed up in my lap and snuggled in my arms as we talked. After a few minutes, I suggested that we pray.

"Father God," I prayed, "we come to You in the name that is above every name. We speak to this cancer in the authority of that name and command it to dry up and die. Place Your healing hands on Shane's diseased body and heal him. Restore him to perfect health, and grant him a full and productive life. In the name of Jesus Christ we pray. Amen."

When I arrived home later that evening, my wife met me at the door. "You're never going to believe what happened," she said, her voice brimming with excitement.

She went on to tell me that when Rick and Chris returned home, Chris proceeded to change the bandage covering the cancerous tumor on Shane's cheek. When she did, a huge piece of it fell out in her hand.

The following Sunday I preached three morning services and then went directly to the airport to catch a flight to Alaska. When I finally landed in Anchorage, several hours later, I called home to let Brenda know that I had arrived. As soon as she heard my voice, she started talking excitedly. "The rest of the tumor fell out," she said.

"Slow down," I said, "and start at the beginning."

"When Rick and Chris got home from church this morning, it was time for Chris to change the dressing on Shane's cheek. When she removed the bandage, the rest of the tumor fell out in her hand. The cancer had dried up and died, just like you prayed it would."

That was more than fifteen years ago, and Shane is an adult now and still cancer free! Thank God that Rick and Chris not only sought the best medical care available, but also turned to the Lord in the hour of their need. And more importantly, thank God that "Jesus Christ is the same yesterday and today and forever."[66]

5. The account of the Syrophenician woman reminds us that a parent's love is but a dim reflection of our heavenly Father's love for us.

Being a father myself, I know the feelings a father has for his children. Nothing pains me more than seeing my daughter suffer, nor does anything bless me more than her happiness. Whatever touches her touches me. If I, a mere mortal, have these kinds of feelings for my daughter, then I can only imagine how much more Father God cares for His children. Well did Jesus say, "If you, then, though you are evil, know how to give good gifts to your children, how much more will your Father in heaven give good gifts to those who ask him!"[67]

I am especially sensitive to this truth at the present time because my daughter is going through a difficult season in her life. She was recently diagnosed with systematic lupus and being the mother of two small children, this has put a tremendous strain on the family. No matter what I am doing, Leah's situation is never far from my mind. When I lie in bed at night awaiting sleep, my mind is searching for solutions. My first thought upon waking in the morning is a prayer for her. When I pray, her needs take precedence over almost everything else. I am her father, and I am touched by the feelings of her infirmities. What hurts her hurts me. Her pain is my pain.

Is not my concern for Leah but a dim reflection of the Father's concern for His own? Isn't this what He is talking about when He says, "'Can a woman forget her nursing child, And not have compassion on the son of her womb?

Surely they may forget, Yet I will not forget you. See, I have inscribed you on the palms of My hands...."[68]

It is nearly inconceivable that a nursing mother could forget the child at her breast after all she went through to bring that new life into the world. That tiny bundle of humanity, so fragile, so dependent, is flesh of her flesh. Surely nothing short of death itself could make her forget her precious child. Yet in extreme cases mothers have been known to forsake their children. It is unnatural. It goes against everything that a mother is. Still it does happen.

But Father God could never forget one of His own. He has made us a part of Himself. We are engraved on the palms of His hands. As Matthew Henry notes in his biblical commentary, "God's compassions to his people infinitely exceed those of the tenderest parents towards their children. What are the affections of nature to those of the God of nature!"[69]

No matter what you are facing right now be encouraged. The One who intervened on behalf of the Syrophenician woman and her daughter will help you. He sees your situation. He hears your desperate cries. He cares about you and those you love. And He is coming to deliver you from your crisis. "Do not fear, little flock, for it is your Father's good pleasure to give you the kingdom."[70]

CHAPTER EIGHT

The Man Born Blind

John 9:1-38

THE STREETS SURROUNDING THE TEMPLE are thronged with pilgrims who have come to celebrate the Feast of Tabernacles. Although I cannot see them, having been blind from birth, I sense their nearness. Shamelessly I beg for alms, while banging my cup on the stone pavers near the temple gate. "Have pity upon me." I cry, "He who gives to the poor lends to the Lord. God Himself will repay him."[71]

Footsteps draw near and a heavy coin clangs into my cup. "Bless you," I say. Lifting my voice I call to those who are hurrying by, "Blessed is he who considers the poor. The Lord will deliver him in the time of trouble."[72]

After a while the foot traffic thins out and I lean back against the wall. Turning my face to the sky to enjoy the warmth of the sun, I thank God for His blessings. Although I am blind, I refuse to feel sorry for myself, having decided early on that self-pity was a luxury I simply could not afford.

I listen as a familiar cadre of beggars gather near the gate. With one voice they bemoan their unhappy plight. They are a sad lot, to be sure—deaf, mute, crippled, and maimed—but these are not their most debilitating handicaps. No, the thing that makes them so tragic is the lie they tell themselves. Instead of seeing themselves as persons of worth and dignity, created in the image of God, they define themselves by their handicap. One thinks of himself as a cripple, another considers himself a mute. Not one of them thinks of himself as a man.

It's not that I'm insensitive to their plight, for I have had to deal with the same temptations my entire life. It would be easy enough to give in to self-pity; after all my whole life has been lived in darkness. Never have I seen the light of day or raindrops glistening on the petals of a flower. Never have I seen my mother's face or the color of her hair. Never have I read a book or seen the beauty of the moon over water at night. Never have I seen a young maiden smile at me with desire in her eyes or had the opportunity to consider the possibility of marriage and a family of my own. Never have I known what it is like to roam the countryside or to explore the world or to contemplate a career other than begging.

If the truth be known, self-pity is a siren whose song forever tempts me, but I refuse to succumb. I am blind, but I am not dead! Although I cannot see, not even my hand in front of my face, many of the pleasures of life are still available to me. For instance, I have a very discerning palate and I take great pleasure in the simple flavors others hardly notice. A fine meal and good conversation never fail to delight me. I love listening to the accounts of merchants who have come from afar. Their colorful descriptions become my eyes and through them I am able to see the world.

If I allowed myself to succumb to self-pity, I would be worse off, not better. It would blind me in ways the loss of my sight never could.

Hearing the sound of several people approaching, I am instantly alert. They stop a few feet from where I am sitting, but I sense their interest. Although the traffic in the street is noisy and they are speaking in hushed tones, I have no trouble distinguishing their words. One of them must be a teacher for someone asks, "Rabbi, who sinned, this man or his parents, that he was born blind?"

Ah, a question with which I am only too familiar. Before making peace with my predicament, I must have asked myself the same thing at least a million times. As far as I am concerned, it is a question without an answer. Surely I am not being punished for something I did before I was born. How could that be? And what kind of God would punish an innocent child for the sins of his parents? Besides even if I could figure out why I was born blind, it wouldn't change a thing. I would still be blind!

Nonetheless, I am surprised by the Teacher's answer. "Neither this man nor his parents sinned. This happened so that the work of God might be displayed in his life."

Now that's a departure from traditional thinking. The Pharisees and the teachers of the Law are strong proponents of the law of cause and effect. As far as they are concerned, sickness and disease are never random. To their way of thinking, someone is always to blame.

For my parents, that has been a burden nearly too heavy to bear. The mere sight of me invokes a nameless guilt that leaves them mute with grief. As a consequence, they have been forced to distance themselves from me in order to survive.

Hearing movement, I sense that the Teacher has squatted down near me. He spits into the dust, and I hear Him scraping in the dirt. Now His hands are upon my face, and He is caking my eyes with the mud that He has fashioned from His saliva. Before I can demand an explanation He says, "Go wash in the Pool of Siloam."

Being an independent sort, I am not accustomed to taking orders, but there is an authority in His voice that I do not question. Without hesitating I get to my feet and turn toward the street. Although I cannot see, I have had a lifetime to adapt to my blindness, and I traverse the familiar streets with little difficulty. Arriving at the Pool of Siloam, I make my way to the edge of the water where I kneel.

Before plunging my face into the water to wash, I pause, wondering what this is all about. I have heard many things about this Teacher called Jesus. Some say that He is a healer, that He has even opened the eyes of the blind.[73] Could it be that I am to receive my sight? The mere thought is nearly impossible to comprehend, yet I find that it has taken possession of my mind. My heart is beating a heavy rhythm in my chest, and I am nearly sick with excitement.

At last I plunge my face into the water and begin scrubbing the mud from my eyes. Something is happening, of that I am sure. Already I see flashes of light and a rainbow of colors dance behind my tightly closed lids. Having never seen either light or colors, I find that I am trembling with anticipation. Lifting my head, I brush the water from my face and open my eyes.

"Oh," I gasp, stunned by the brilliance of the light.

Staggering to my feet, I look around in amazement, dazed by all I see. The streets are crowded with people and I marvel at their diversity—the delicate shading of their skin and the color of their hair. In the distance the temple towers gleam against the blue of the sky, while overhead birds dart and soar. A breath of a breeze brushes my face, and the leaves of a nearby tree reflect the light as they move in the wind.

Kneeling once more I study my own reflection in the still water. *So this is what I look like,* I muse. My hair is darker than I had imagined and coarse as I knew it would be. The sun and the wind have weathered my face, leaving it dark and wrinkled well beyond my years. My beard is ragged and matted, in need of grooming.

Now I study my own hands, noticing the texture of my skin, the way it wrinkles over my knuckles and the pattern my blood veins make. Noticing several dark blotches on my skin, I decide they must be what I have heard others refer to as age spots. Turning my hands palm up, I examine the delicate configuration of lines, marveling at the intricate designs they make.

Suddenly I think of my parents and what the miracle of my sight will mean to them. Leaping to my feet, I hurry through the streets toward their home. Turning a final corner, I suddenly find myself confronted by a group of neighbors. Although I have never seen them, I immediately recognize them by their voices. They stare at me in dumbfounded amazement, as if they cannot believe their eyes. Recognition fills their faces, but reason tells them it can't be. Finally one of them says, "Isn't this the same man who used to sit and beg? Isn't he the one who was born blind?"

In an instant they are all talking at once. "He's one and the same," asserts a small man. "I would know him anywhere."

Something is happening, of that I am sure. I find that I am trembling with anticipation.

"It can't be him," says another. "This man can see."

"It's him all right," declares a third man. "Look at him. I would know that face anywhere."

"No, it's not him," argues another. "It can't be."

"It is, I tell you. It's him."

"No, this fellow just looks like the blind beggar, that's all."

"Quiet," I holler. "Quiet!"

When the voices subside I declare, "I am the man. I was born blind, but now I see!"

"How can that be?" they demand, all of them talking at once. "How were your eyes opened?"

"The man they call Jesus made some mud and put it on my eyes. He told me to go to the pool and wash. So I went and washed, and then I could see."

Rather than praising God for His mighty works, they struggle to comprehend how this can be. Desperately they try to figure out how a man who was born blind can now see. Finally they give up. What Jesus has done for me is simply beyond the realm of their experience. They have no frame of reference, no way to understand a miracle of this magnitude.

"Let's consult the Pharisees," suggests an old man. "Maybe they can shed some light on this remarkable event."

Although I protest it does no good. Reluctantly I allow myself to be talked into going with them. In short order, I find myself being questioned by the Pharisees. Once more I tell my story, leaving nothing out. To my amazement they are not impressed. That I can see matters not a whit to them. The fact that all of this took place on the Sabbath seems to be more important than my healing.

"This Jesus is not from God," declares one of the Pharisees, "for He does not keep the Sabbath."

"How can you say that?" asks another. "Can a sinner do miraculous signs like this?"

They continue to argue among themselves, but I soon lose interest. My thoughts return to the One they call Jesus, to the One who gave me my sight. Sitting at the temple gate day after day, I have heard His name bantered about. He must be a remarkable teacher for I have heard nothing but rave reviews. Once, I am told, the Pharisees sent the temple guards to arrest Him. When they returned empty-handed, the chief priests demanded an explanation. "Why didn't you bring Him in?" they asked. Shaking their heads in awe, the guards simply said, "No one ever spoke the way this man does."[74]

Some say He is the promised Messiah. Pointing to His numerous miracles they reason, "When the Christ comes, will he do more miraculous signs than this man?"[75] Others say He can't be the Christ for He comes from Galilee. "Does not the Scripture say," they reason, "that the Christ will come from David's family and from Bethlehem, the town where David lived?"[76]

My musings are interrupted by the arrival of my parents. Having never seen them before this moment, I study them intently. To my surprise I discover that my father is an old man. His shoulders are bowed with weariness, and his steps are slow and uncertain. Mother clings tightly to his arm, her eyes downcast. She casts a furtive glance toward me but quickly looks away when she sees me looking at her. Shame colors her face and guilt too.

Life has obviously taken a heavy toll on them, and they seem more than a little cowed by their appearance before the Pharisees. Obviously they know what is at stake here, and they do not want to be put out of the synagogue.

"Is this your son?" barks one of the Jews. "Was he born blind?"

"Yes," my father answers in a small voice, while my mother nods her head in agreement.

"If he was born blind," demands another, "how is it that he can now see?"

The man's tone is derisive, infuriating my father. As I watch, he seems to gather himself and something of the man he once was asserts itself. "We know he is our son," he says, "and we know he was born blind. But how he can see now, or who opened his eyes, we don't know."

Just as quickly his anger fades and now he seems to shrink before my eyes. Nodding toward me, he continues in an apologetic tone, "Why don't you ask him? He is of age; he will speak for himself."

Without waiting to be dismissed, he takes my mother by the arm and slowly makes his way through the crowd. I follow them with my eyes, but they do not look back or acknowledge me in any way. Although I am no longer blind, it seems I am still making life difficult for them. Their pain grieves me in a way I cannot put into words, and

I would do almost anything to make their life better if only I could.

Turning toward me, the Pharisee continues in his overbearing tone, "Give glory to God," he says. "Admit that this Jesus is a sinner."

"Who am I to judge whether He is a sinner or not? The only thing I know is that I was blind and now I see!"

My answer seems to agitate them and they whisper among themselves. It is obvious to me that they have no desire to know the truth. Their minds are already made up and as far as they are concerned, Jesus is a troublemaker and a fraud.

Once more they press me for the details of my healing. Impatiently I reply, "I have told you already and you did not listen. Why do you want to hear it again? Do you want to become His disciples, too?"

I have touched a nerve and they angrily demand, "Who do you think you are to instruct us? You are ignorant and unlearned!"

Raising my voice above theirs, I press my advantage. "You were the ones who taught us that God listens only to Godly men who do His will, so how can you now say this

Man is a sinner? He is the only Man who has ever opened the eyes of a man born blind. If He is not from God, how can He do such a thing?"

Their faces are full of anger and they are gnashing their teeth at me. "You were steeped in sin at birth," they scream, "how dare you lecture us!"

Suddenly they are all around me, pushing and shoving. Someone tries to gouge me in the eye while someone else pushes me from behind. I stumble forward trying desperately to maintain my balance. If I were to fall, they might trample me underfoot.

Reaching the street they put me out of the synagogue, not just physically but spiritually as well. They excommunicate me, cutting me off from the whole congregation of Israel. They have made me a pariah, an outcast!

Standing in the street outside the synagogue, I cannot help thinking that things have hardly turned out the way I would have expected. Instead of bringing joy, the healing of my eyes has loosed a firestorm of controversy. Worst of all, it has confused and frightened my parents as much as ever my blindness did. Instead of healing the breach in our relationship, it has served only to further alienate them from me.

Turning to go I find myself face-to-face with the Man who opened my eyes. Though I have never seen His face, I know who He is, and in spite of all I have been through, my spirit leaps within me. There is something about Him that warms my heart, that draws me to Him.

The contrast between Him and the Pharisees is stark. His face is full of kindness while their faces are full of anger. He is filled with light while they are altogether dark. They rejected me. He has sought me out. They were judgmental. He is accepting, forgiving.

Looking me in the eyes, He asks, "Do you believe in the Son of Man, the promised Messiah?"

"I want to believe. If I knew who He was, I am sure I would believe."

"You know who He is, you just haven't realized it yet."

For the second time today, He has opened my eyes and my understanding, too. Now I see Him, I mean really see Him, and I know who He is—the Son of Man, the promised Messiah! Not just a teacher, or even a prophet as I had thought, but the promised One.

Falling to my knees, I worship Him. "Lord, I believe. I truly believe that You are the Son of God."

Life Lessons

LIFE LESSONS

The Man Born Blind

JOHN BEGINS HIS ACCOUNT OF this miracle with a question: "Rabbi, who sinned, this man or his parents, that he was born blind?"[77] Today we might ask, "What did this man do to deserve such a fate? How could this happen?" No matter how the question is phrased it is as old as our race and can be reduced to a single word—"why."

Most of us realize that even if we could know "why" it wouldn't change a thing, so why is it so important to us? Could it be that we want to believe we live in an orderly world where cause and effect reign supreme, where good is rewarded and evil is punished? Could it be because we want to believe that in an orderly world there would be no random tragedies, no indiscriminate disease or death? Could it be because in an orderly world we feel that we would have more control over our fate?

The religious teachers of Jesus' day believed in just such a world, an orderly world of cause and effect. "The general principle was laid down by R. Ammi: 'There is no death without sin, and there is no suffering without iniquity.'"[78]

As far as the rabbis were concerned, there was always a direct correlation between personal sin and sickness. According to their teachings, either this man or his parents had sinned. There was no other explanation.

Yet such teachings had to be troubling to any thinking person. How could a person sin before being born? And what kind of a God would punish a child for the parents' sins? "Yet the Rabbis held such things to be possible. There are sayings which speak of children as being born epileptic or leprous on account of the sins of their parents. The untimely death of a scholar [they believed] can be ascribed to his mother's dalliance with idolatry while pregnant with him."[79]

Today we shake our heads at such primitive beliefs, yet we too have developed elaborate belief systems to "protect" ourselves. There are those who teach, by implication if not by precept, that a true believer need not suffer from sickness or disease. And if he does it must be because he does not have enough faith, or he is out of the will of God, or there is sin in his life.

While there are instances where personal sin causes sickness and even death—for example, promiscuous sexual behavior may result in a sexually transmitted disease or driving while intoxicated may result in an auto accident that leaves the driver a quadriplegic—all sickness is not a direct result of personal sin. Nor is good health necessarily the result of a sinless life.

After nearly forty years in Christian ministry, it is my considered opinion that sin is responsible for disease and death. That is not to say that this man was born blind because of his personal sin, or even, God forbid, the sin of his parents. Rather, it means that sin has tainted the entire human race, and disease and death are the inevitable consequences. Romans 5:12 (KJV) declares: "Wherefore, as by one man sin entered into the world, and death by sin; and so death passed upon all men...."

We inhabit a planet that is in rebellion, and we are part of a race living outside of God's will. One consequence of that rebellion is sickness and death. God doesn't send this plague upon people, nor does He will it. It is simply a natural consequence of humanity's fallen state. Although as believers we are new creations in Christ,[80] we remain a part of this human family. As a consequence, we too suffer the inevitable repercussions of that fallen state, even though we may be personally committed to the doing of God's will and the coming of His kingdom.

When sickness or tragedy strikes, we long for a reason, an explanation, but often there is none. In desperation we try to make some sense out of it, but often there is simply no pat answer, no ready conclusion. In times like that, we must always resist the temptation to speak where God has not spoken. Beyond the simple explanation that sickness and death come as a result of humanity's sinful state, God has not given us any insight into the "why" of individual situations.

In the case of this man who was born blind, Jesus redirects our thinking. Instead of focusing on the cause of his blindness, Jesus turns our attention to its purpose—"'...but this happened so that the work of God might be displayed in his life.'"[81] That is not to say that God caused his blindness, but only that He used it to demonstrate His healing power and His mercy.

Some years ago, while I was serving as the senior pastor of Christian Chapel in Tulsa, Oklahoma, I prayed for a lady whose thyroid had died following the birth of her second child. The doctors were treating her with medication, but it was largely ineffective. Her emotions were all over the place, and she found it virtually impossible to function normally.

After prayer she felt so good that she decided to stop taking her prescribed medication. She didn't tell her husband because she knew he would worry. To be on the safe side, she called her doctor and informed him what she had done. Of course, he told her that he couldn't recommend coming off her medication to which she replied, "I understand. The reason for my call is simply precautionary. If I am not healed and I experience a medical emergency, I want you to know that I haven't had any medication since before church on Sunday morning."

At dinner on Friday evening, her husband said, "Thank God the doctors have finally gotten your medication regulated. You've been your old self these past few days."

"There's something I need to tell you," she replied. "It's not the medication. I haven't had any since Sunday morning. God healed me when Pastor prayed for me."

For his peace of mind, her husband insisted that she return to the doctor and repeat the tests on her thyroid. I have copies of both sets of her medical records in my file. The first set says, "Thyroid is dead." The second set says, "Thyroid is normal." Then the doctor wrote, "This is a miracle."

Perhaps you are facing a serious health issue in your own life, or maybe someone you love is. Instead of succumbing to the temptation of the "why" questions—an exercise in futility if ever there was one—let me urge you to make peace with your situation. Surrender it to God and ask Him to redeem it, to use it for His purposes.

Facing a desperate situation, it seems we have three choices. "We can curse life for doing this to us and look for some way to express our grief and rage. Or we can grit our teeth and endure it. Or we can accept it. The first alternative is useless. The second is sterile and exhausting. The third is the only way."[82]

Acceptance is the right choice, not resignation which gives up and says, "Whatever will be, will be." Acceptance believes for a miracle even as you face the reality of your situation. Acceptance does not demand a predetermined conclusion; rather it leaves the nature of the miracle to the wisdom of God. It may come in the form of divine healing or it may come as a miracle in your spirit, enabling you to experience peace and contentment in the midst of your suffering. Either way God is glorified, and His purposes are served.

CHAPTER NINE

Nicodemus

John 3:1-18

AS I MAKE MY WAY through the dark streets toward Gethsemane, my mind is racing. It has been quite a week. In addition to the normal chaos of the annual Passover with its thousands of pilgrims, there was that incident in the Temple. Although I wasn't there, I have heard about it. According to the reports I have received, the Teacher from Nazareth made a whip out of cords and drove the money changers out of the Temple courts.[83]

The Sadducees were understandably upset for they consider the Temple their domain, not to mention the fact that they generate a considerable profit changing money and selling sacrifices. There's no telling what they might have done to Jesus if they had not feared the reaction of the pilgrims. To be honest with you, I must admit that I took no little pleasure in seeing them put in their place. A little Pharisee/Sadducee rivalry no doubt.

What's of more interest to me is the Man himself. Not only is He a remarkable teacher, but He also has the power to do miracles.[84] Among my peers He is the subject of considerable controversy; in fact, He has succeeded in dividing the Sanhedrin. Some of the more radical members believe He is demon-possessed. They claim His miraculous powers come from the devil.[85] I believe otherwise. At times I have even wondered if He might be the promised Messiah.

Which brings me to the purpose of my nocturnal meanderings—I am on my way to meet with this Jesus of Nazareth. I have been told that He often goes to Gethsemane or to the Mount of Olives for solitude. If my information is correct, I may be able to have a private conversation with Him.

My purpose for approaching Him in this manner is purely pragmatic. He is so popular with the common people that it would be virtually impossible to have any kind of a private conversation under different circumstances. Not to mention the fact that I have no desire to alienate any of my colleagues on the Sanhedrin. At some point that may become unavoidable, but for the time being I would like to keep my pilgrimage confidential.

The moon is full and high in the sky as I approach Gethsemane, causing the trees to cast deformed shadows on the ground. As I enter the garden I pause to listen. At first

all I hear is the sound of my own breathing, loud in my ears. As my ears adjust to
the stillness of the night, I begin to discern
sounds—the breeze in the trees, a small
animal rustling in the brush, and the noise
of insects. Faintly I hear the sound of a
Man's voice, the words indistinguishable
to my ear.

Following the sound, I make my way
through the garden until I come to an
open space. He is kneeling in the clearing
with His face lifted toward the heavens.
Obviously He is praying, but I have never
witnessed prayer like this. There is no
posturing, no careful turning of a phrase.
Instead, there is a camaraderie, an inti-
macy in His prayer that generates a
hunger in my own heart, an ache really.
Would that I knew God the way He does.

The thought of intruding on such an
intimate moment is unacceptable to me,
but before I can slip away He senses my
presence. Rising from the place of prayer,

Recognition fills
His face, and He
takes me by the
shoulders and
greets me.

He moves across the clearing toward me. Recognition fills His face, and He takes me by the shoulders and greets me with a kiss.

"Nicodemus," He says, "how good of you to come."

The warmth of His greeting gives me pause. It is almost as if He were expecting me. Yet, that could not be for I discussed my plans with no one, not even my wife. For a moment I am at a loss for words, but with an effort I recover my composure.

Clearing my throat I begin, nervousness causing me to rush my words. "Rabbi, we know You are a special teacher sent from God. There's no other explanation. I mean, how else could You do the miracles You are doing?"

He studies me intently, as if trying to discern my motives. Finally He says, "I tell you the absolute truth and I do not exaggerate, you will never see the kingdom of God, let alone enter it, unless you are born again."

"Born again! What in the world are You talking about? I'm a grown man. I can't return to my mother's womb and be born a second time. Teacher, I respect You, but You are not making sense."

"Nicodemus, don't take My words so literal. I'm not talking about returning to your mother's womb. I'm talking about being born of the Spirit. There is a natural birth and there is a spiritual birth. The natural birth produces physical life, and the spiritual birth produces spiritual life. The natural birth can never produce spiritual life, and without spiritual life you will never enter the kingdom of God."

What He is saying makes a certain kind of sense, although I am having trouble getting my mind around it. The natural birth is easy enough to understand, but what in the world is spiritual birth? How does it happen? What does a person look like when he is born of the Spirit? Is he two people or one? And if he is only one person, which one is he—the natural man or the spiritual man?

My confusion must be apparent for He says, "What I am talking about can't be understood until you've experienced it. Spiritual truth comes to the heart first. Even then, even when you know it is more real than anything you have ever experienced, you will still have trouble comprehending it, let alone explaining it. It's kind of like the wind. You know it is real even though you can't explain it. You hear the sound it makes when it blows, but you don't know where it comes from or where it is going.

"You are a learned man, Nicodemus, a teacher in Israel, and yet you do not know God. Why? Because you have created a religion of rules. You study the Law, but you do not know the Lawgiver. You know all about Him, but you don't know Him.

"What God wants, more than anything, is a relationship with you. Why do you think He sent His only begotten Son into the world? Not to condemn the world I can tell you that, but that through Him the world might be saved.

"Stop trusting in the Law. Stop trusting in your own efforts. Throw yourself on the love of God, for He loved the world so much that He gave His only Son that you might have eternal life.

"If you believe in Me and the things I am telling you, you will not be judged and found wanting. But if you do not believe, you are already judged and found wanting for you have not believed in God's one and only Son."

Having said that Jesus slips into the night, leaving me with my thoughts, and what a hodgepodge they are. My purpose in coming tonight was to get some answers, but what I have been left with is a whole new set of questions. Has my entire life been wasted? Does my devotion to the

Law of Moses count for nothing? Where do I go from here? What do I do now?

Although I am more than a little confused, there is no denying what I feel when I am in His presence. He gives me hope. When He speaks, life seems to open up. It's filled with possibilities. Studying the Law, on the other hand, leaves me feeling like a failure. No matter how hard I try I can never measure up.

If I am honest with myself, I have to admit that the Law is out of reach. Is that what Jesus is trying to get me to see? That since I can never fully keep the Law, it will always be a source of condemnation. And even if I could fully obey the Law from this moment forward, which of course I can't, it would not remove the sinful failures of my past. Maybe that is the ultimate purpose of the Law—to convince me of my need in a Savior.

Being an intellectual, I have always approached God cognitively, but it hasn't

There is no denying what I feel when I am in His presence. He gives me hope.

really worked. I know a lot about God, but I don't know Him. He is an abstraction to me, a theological concept at best, nothing more.

If I understand Jesus correctly, He is telling me the way to find God is relationally, the way a child knows his parents or the way a man relates to his wife. As a child, I knew my parents because I was in relationship with them—I lived in their home, I ate at their table. There were family rules of course, but I never mistook the rules for my parents.

Is that what I have done with God? Have I mistaken the Law for the Lawgiver? So it would seem and what a fine mess I have made. As men go, I am a morally good man, but I have no relationship with God. So where do I go from here?

Maybe it all boils down to what Jesus called being born again. Maybe the only way I can ever really know God is to be born into His family, to live in His house, and eat at His table. If I could do that, then maybe I could pray the way Jesus prayed—as if I were having an intimate conversation. As if God were nearer than the breath I breathe and more real than life itself.

The sun is pushing the darkness from the eastern sky as I get to my feet and turn toward the city. I am still troubled and there is much I do not understand, but I am optimistic. Hope burns in my heart. Who knows but what I might be born again.

Life Lessons

LIFE LESSONS

Nicodemus

UNLIKE MANY OF THE PEOPLE to whom Jesus ministered, Nicodemus was a learned man, a teacher of Israel and a member of the Jewish ruling council, the Sanhedrin. He was a wealthy man and influential, wise and highly respected by his peers. That he became a follower of Jesus seems apparent. On at least one occasion, he spoke in defense of Jesus saying, "Does our law condemn anyone without first hearing him to find out what he is doing?"[86] And following the crucifixion of Jesus, he brought seventy-five pounds of myrrh and aloes and joined Joseph of Arimathea in preparing our Lord's body for burial.[87]

I mention all of this because it is sometimes easy to mistakenly assume that it is only life's rejects who need Jesus, only those who have made a mess of their lives. Of course, nothing could be further from the truth—we all need Him—young and old, rich and poor, churched and unchurched.

Nicodemus was a pious man, a devout Jew, a teacher in Israel and yet after years of faithful service, he still hungered for something more. Had he not heard Jesus speaking of God and His kingdom, had he not seen the miracles Jesus did, he might have lived his whole life without ever addressing the longing in his soul. But having seen and heard, having been in the presence of Jesus, he could no longer ignore the ache within. Once he saw evidence that it was possible to experience God in a life-changing way, he could not rest. Desperate to know God in a personal way, he risked everything by seeking a private audience with Jesus.

There are a lot of reasons why religion can never satisfy, but the one core reason is that religion misunderstands the problem. It focuses on the Law—the keeping of rules. But the problem isn't that we have broken the rules (though we have). The real problem is a broken relationship. When we sin we don't just break the rules, we break trust with God and separate ourselves from Him, spiritually and relationally.

Donald Miller tells of a friend whose wife was unfaithful to him. This friend overheard his wife on the phone with another man. He heard her confess her love and enjoyment of the other man's touch. Stumbling out of the house, he drove around Baltimore in a daze. He sat in coffee shops with his head in his hands. He bought a bus ticket to Pittsburgh but missed his bus because he was sick from smoking a pack of cigarettes. For an hour he vomited yellow muck into a filthy toilet in the men's room at the bus station.[88]

Likening the fall of man[89] to the betrayal of his friend, Miller writes, "I think God must have felt like my friend in Baltimore. I think it was something terribly painful for God to endure...You wouldn't think God would forgive them at all. You would think God would just kill them. If a couple of terrorists pulled something like that today, they might be dragged through the streets, their bodies used as human torches and hung in a public place for months. People would travel from miles away to spit on their bones."[90]

But that's not how God responds. Grieved and heartbroken, He seeks reconciliation rather than revenge. As Miller points out, "The God of the Bible seems to be brokenhearted over the separation in our relationship and downright obsessed with mending the tear."[91] The truth is, God loves us so much that He is willing to take the rap for us in order to restore the relationship.[92] All we have to do is trust in the finished work of Christ and call on the name of the Lord.[93]

Another thing we learn from Nicodemus' encounter with Jesus is that no one is condemned because of the sinful things they have done, but because of what they didn't do. Jesus put it like this: "...but whoever does not believe stands condemned already because he has not believed in the name of God's one and only Son."[94]

The late Rich Mullins (well-known Christian artist and songwriter) was hiking the Appalachian Trail when he had a chance encounter with a man who professed to be gay. Here's what happened. Having been on the trail for some days, Rich was hungry for a real meal so he hiked into town. While having dinner in a small cafe, he struck up a conversation with a fellow diner. When he finished his coffee, the man offered to drive him back to the trail. Since it was nearly dark and a five-mile hike back to the camp-ground, Rich accepted the offer.

Once they were in the car the man said, "I suppose I should tell you that I'm gay."

Rich responded, "I guess I should tell you that I'm a Christian."

Slowing the car, the man asked, "Do you want to get out?"

"Not unless you're throwing me out. Why do you ask?"

"I don't know. I thought Christians hated gays."

"That's funny," Rich said, "I thought Christians were supposed to love everybody."

They drove in silence for a minute or two, the only sounds being the whir of the tires on the asphalt and the rush of the wind past the windows. Finally the driver said, "I guess you think I'm going to hell because I'm gay," to which Rich replied, "No one goes to hell because of the things they do. People go to hell because of what they didn't do, because they reject the grace that God so longs to give us, regardless of what we have done."[95]

If that's true, and I believe it is based on what Jesus told Nicodemus (John 3:18), then it behooves me to ask you if you have allowed God to love you? Have you received His love gift? Have you received the Lord Jesus Christ as your personal Savior?

If you haven't, there is no better time. Romans 10:9-10 says, "...if you confess with your mouth, 'Jesus is Lord,' and believe in your heart that God raised him from the dead, you will be saved. For it is with your heart that you believe and are justified, and it is with your mouth that you confess and are saved."

CHAPTER TEN

The Two on the Road to Emmaus

Luke 24:13-35

CLEOPAS AND I ARE RETURNING from Jerusalem to Emmaus, a journey of about threescore furlongs. Normally he is a gregarious companion, but today he is locked in a sorrowful silence. Studying him out of the corner of my eye, I take note of how dramatically he has aged. His step is slow, uncertain; his shoulders bent beneath an unseen burden. In his eyes I see a grief that mirrors my own, and his face is a suffering mask. Placing my hand on his shoulder as we walk, I search for a word of comfort but find that I have nothing to say. Even the eternal Scriptures seem mute before the evil that has turned our holy city into a house of horrors.

To my surprise, I discover that grief blinds you or at the very least it distorts your vision; it makes it impossible for you to see things clearly. I mean, the wonderful things Jesus said and did have not changed but grief has rendered them unreal. Now all I can remember is the awful way He died. I cannot get the tragically grotesque images out of my mind. What transpired has shaken me to the core of my soul. My faith in human nature has been shattered, maybe even my faith in God.

Once more I review the events in my mind. On the first day of the week, Cleopas and I journeyed to Jerusalem for the Passover, arriving just as Jesus was entering the city. Pilgrims thronged the streets and the air resounded with their joyous shouts. "Blessed is the King who comes in the name of the Lord!" Others were crying, "Peace in Heaven and glory in the highest!"

Of course, our hearts leaped within us and we lifted our voices to join theirs. Having heard His teachings and seen His miracles, we were convinced that He was more than a prophet. In our hearts, we truly believed He was the promised Messiah. Being among His earliest followers, we hoped to have a few minutes with Him sometime during Passover week, but of course that wasn't to be. We consoled ourselves by spending time with others who loved Him as much as we did. We exchanged stories of His miracles and talked of things to come.

Lazarus invited us to share the Passover meal with him and his two sisters in Bethany. Awaking the next morning, we learned that Jesus was in the custody of the Romans who were preparing to crucify Him. We rushed to the place of execution, but there was nothing we could do. By mid-afternoon it was over. Jesus was dead—crucified like a common criminal. And when He died, our hopes and dreams died with Him.

As we are discussing these unspeakable events, a stranger falls into step beside us. Being in no mood for companionship, I ignore Him, as does Cleopas. After a while the silence grows uncomfortable and the stranger asks, "What were you discussing when I joined you? From the looks on your faces, it must have been serious."

Stopping, Cleopas turns to Him. "Have you just arrived in Jerusalem? Do you know nothing of the terrible things that have happened here?"

"What things?"

"There was a gross miscarriage of justice involving Jesus of Nazareth, a Prophet who did many miracles and amazed everyone with His teaching. One of His own disciples betrayed Him to our chief priests and rulers, who, out of envy, falsely accused Him and sentenced Him to death. Since the Romans reserve the right of capital punishment to themselves, our leaders turned Him over to them to be crucified."

Pausing for a moment to regain control of his emotions, Cleopas shakes his head sadly. "We truly believed Jesus was the promised Messiah, the One who was going to redeem Israel. Now we don't know what to believe.

"To further complicate things, His remains have disappeared. Early this morning some of our women went to the tomb to anoint His body for burial and the tomb was empty. His body was gone! They claimed to have seen a vision of angels who told them not to seek the living among the dead—whatever that is supposed to mean.

"I would like to believe He's alive, I really would, but I can't. I saw what the Romans did to Him. No man could survive that kind of butchery."

Having said that, Cleopas resumes walking and I with him. After a moment the stranger hurries to rejoin us. "Maybe there is another way of looking at these things," He says. "Maybe this is not a tragedy, but just part of God's eternal plan."

We look at Him as if He has lost His mind, but He simply says, "Hear me out. You are heartbroken because He was betrayed by one of His own[96] and yet isn't that a fulfillment of Scripture? Is it not written of Him, 'Even my close friend, whom I trusted, he who shared my bread, has lifted up his heel against me'?[97]

"And though the religious leaders spit in His face and struck Him with their hands,[98] more than seven hundred years ago the prophet Isaiah said it was going to be like that. According to his prophecy, the Messiah testifies, 'I offered my back to those who beat me, my cheeks to those who pulled out my beard; I did not hide my face from mocking and spitting.'[99]

"Was He beaten beyond all recognition? The prophet said it would be so: '...his appearance was so disfigured beyond that of any man and his form marred beyond human likeness...'[100]

"Was He mocked and scorned?[101] That too was prophesied, 'All who see me mock me; they hurl insults, shaking their heads: He trusts in the LORD; let the LORD. . .deliver him, since he delights in him.'"[102]

Cleopas and I look at each other in dumbfounded amazement. Is it possible that all of this was truly part of God's eternal plan? Was Jesus a willing sacrifice rather than a helpless captive? Could it be?

My mind is racing, recalling things that Jesus said that seemed to make no sense when He spoke them. "I lay down my life for the sheep. No one takes it from me, but I lay it down of my own accord. I have authority to lay it down and authority to take it up again."[103]

Another time He tried to tell us that He was going to suffer many things at the hands of the elders, chief priests, and teachers of the Law, and that He would be killed and on the third day be raised to life.[104] At the time we simply dismissed His words, but seen in the light of recent events they take on a new significance.

The stranger is speaking again, expounding the ancient Scriptures with an authority unlike anything we have ever heard. "You are outraged because the heartless Roman soldiers gambled for His garments. Don't be. They were merely fulfilling what was prophesied by the psalmist: 'They divide my garments among them and cast lots for my clothing.'[105]

"Jesus is the suffering servant of whom Isaiah wrote: 'He had no beauty or majesty to attract us to him, nothing in his appearance that we should desire him. He was despised and rejected by men, a man of sorrows, and familiar with suffering. Like one from whom men hide their faces he was despised, and we esteemed him not. But he was pierced for our transgressions, he was crushed for our iniquities; the punishment that brought us peace was upon him, and by his wounds we are healed. We all, like sheep, have gone astray, each of us has turned to his own way; and the LORD has laid on him the iniquity of us all....Yet it was the LORD's will to crush him and cause him to suffer, and though the LORD makes his life a guilt offering, he will see his offspring and prolong his days.... After the suffering of his soul, he will see the light of life and be satisfied; by his knowledge my righteous servant will justify many, and he will bear their iniquities.... For he bore the sin of many, and made intercession for the transgressors.'"[106]

By now the afternoon is well spent and we are not far from Emmaus. We fall into a companionable silence, and I contemplate all that we have heard. The despair that weighed so heavily upon me earlier is mostly gone, replaced by a tentative hope. Unconsciously I find that I am slowing my pace in order to lengthen the journey. There is something so invigorating about the stranger's presence that I don't want our trip to end.

Still, I am troubled. From a child I have been taught that the Messiah was going to be the Deliverer of Israel and that He was going to sit on the throne of His father David. How do I reconcile that with all that I have heard today?

Clearing my throat, I address the stranger. "How does all of this fit in with what we have been taught about the Messiah? Did not the prophets say that of the increase of His government there would be no end and that He would reign on David's throne forever?"[107]

Nodding vigorously Cleopas adds, "Wasn't it Daniel the prophet who said, 'His dominion is an everlasting dominion that will not pass away, and his kingdom is one that will never be destroyed'?"[108]

"You are right of course, but that is only one part of the Messianic prophecies. The Messiah is both a suffering Savior and a conquering King. All of this was prophesied hundreds of years before He came. As a suffering Savior, He was born of a virgin,[109] in Bethlehem,[110] the city of David. Being warned of an angel, His parents fled with Him to Egypt.[111] After Herod died they returned from Egypt and lived in Nazareth.[112] He was rejected by His own people[113] and crucified,[114] and He rose from the dead on the third day.[115]

"When He comes the second time, He will come as a conquering King,[116] and He will fulfill the remainder of the

Messianic prophecies. He will not come as the Son of Man to suffer and die but as the Ancient of Days to sit in judgment and to establish His kingdom."[117]

My mind is racing as I consider the far-reaching ramifications of the stranger's interpretation of the ancient Scriptures. If He's right, and I'm beginning to believe He is, then our whole worldview has been upside down. Maybe the crucifixion was not a disaster, maybe Jesus isn't dead. Maybe He really has risen from the dead.

Topping a final hill we see Emmaus spread out before us, its muted colors looking almost beautiful in the soft light of early evening. Compared to the noisy bustle of Jerusalem it offers a quiet retreat, a needed reprieve, especially after the trauma of the last few days. As we traverse the familiar streets leading to our modest home, I feel the tension draining out of me. It will be good to sleep in my own bed again and to return to the routine of our normal life.

Sensing that we are nearing our destination, the stranger prepares to bid us good-bye before continuing His journey. Cleopas will not hear of it. "Stay with us," he insists. It is late, the day is almost over."

Entering the house he hurries to prepare a basin of water and a towel so our guest can refresh Himself. I go to the kitchen where I put together a simple meal. As I work my mind is considering all we have discussed along the way. Although I am afraid to believe, knowing that I could never survive another disappointment, I find that I cannot refute what the stranger has told us. As unbelievable as it seems, I cannot help thinking that Jesus may be alive.

Placing the bread and the cheese on the table, I join Cleopas and our guest as we prepare to sup. Glancing at Cleopas the stranger asks, "May I have the honor of giving thanks?"

We bow our heads and He begins to pray. When He does the room fills up with the presence of God. This is how I used to feel when I listened to Jesus teaching—as if God himself had drawn near to make Himself known. In His presence I always felt secure, loved. That's how I feel now, and how different it is from the desolation I was feeling before this stranger joined us. I cannot help wondering if He is an angel sent from God to comfort us.

When He finishes praying, He takes the bread and breaks it. As He does, His hands are clearly visible for the first time. I gasp audibly, clinging to the table lest I faint.

Across from me, Cleopas' eyes are wide with amazement. We have both seen the angry red wounds in His hands. There is no mistaking what they are—nail scars.[118] Our guest is no angel. He is none other than Jesus himself!

Before either one of us can say anything, He vanishes. One minute He was there and the next minute He was gone. When He disappeared He took all of our doubts and fears with Him. He is not dead; He has risen! He has conquered death, hell, and the grave.

Leaping to my feet I grab Cleopas and begin dancing around the small room, laughing and crying at the same time. Life will never be the same again, of that I am sure. His resurrection changes everything!

We stumble to a stop gasping for breath, nearly beside ourselves with joy. After a bit Cleopas holds me at arm's length and asks, "Were not our hearts burning within us while he talked with us on the road and opened the Scriptures to us?"[119]

Life Lessons

LIFE LESSONS

The Two on the Road to Emmaus

CLEOPAS AND HIS COMPANION REMIND us how easy it is to miss the truth, even when you are rubbing shoulders with it. Jesus spent at least a half a day with them, and they didn't have a clue who He was. Two things blinded them—grief and their preconceived notions regarding the promised Messiah. Although there are at least 109 messianic prophecies in the Hebrew Scriptures, they were ignorant of many of them. Their teachers taught them only the prophecies that focused on the Messiah as a conquering King—hence when Jesus was crucified, they lost all hope. They were devout Jews and followers of Jesus, but they had no frame of reference in which to understand the Crucifixion and the events surrounding it.

In regards to Jesus being the promised Messiah, there is no evidence more convincing than the fulfilled prophecies.[120] Consider these facts: Every one of the 109 Messianic prophecies was recorded at least 600 years before Jesus was born. Some of them are dated as early as 1,500 years before His birth. These prophecies are far ranging, dealing with both the momentous and the mundane. They range from

His virgin birth[121] to the place of His birth[122] to His earthly ministry[123] to His betrayal[124] and death.[125]

Some may argue that the fulfillment of these prophecies was mere coincidence. Not a very credible argument if you consider the mathematics. "Someone did the math and figured out that the probability of just eight prophecies [not all 109 prophecies] being fulfilled is one chance in one hundred million billion. That number is millions of times greater than the total number of people who've ever walked the planet!"[126]

Perhaps you can grasp the odds better if we illustrate it like this. One hundred million billion silver dollars would cover the state of Texas to a depth of two feet. Now imagine marking one silver dollar and having a blindfolded person wander the whole state and bend down and pick up one coin. What do you think the odds are that the coin picked up would be the marked coin? About the same odds that anybody in history could have fulfilled just eight of the Messianic prophecies.[127]

No thinking person can seriously consider the evidence of fulfilled prophecy and then refute the claims of Christ. They prove beyond all doubt that Jesus is who He claimed to be—the Son of God and the only Savior of our lost race.

It was to these very prophecies that Jesus turned when He set out to rebuild the faith of Cleopas and his companion. "He said to them, 'How foolish you are, and how slow of heart to believe all that the prophets have spoken! Did not the Christ have to suffer these things and then enter his glory?' And beginning with Moses and all the Prophets, he explained to them what was said in all the Scriptures concerning himself."[128]

Unfortunately, it is possible to believe in Jesus intellectually without ever knowing Him personally. What moves a person from mere knowledge to faith is an encounter with Christ. Consider the case of these two despairing disciples. What truth alone could not do, relationship did. When Jesus broke bread with them, something holy happened, and they saw things in a whole different light. The power of His presence moved them from grief-stricken confusion to life-changing faith!

I've had experiences like that, and I'm sure you have too. Experiences that seem ordinary at first glance, but upon closer examination prove otherwise. For instance, when I was sixteen years old, I went swimming in the South Platte River on a hot August afternoon, with a pretty girl who would later become my wife. Carelessly we splashed in the river, oblivious to the sun's deadly rays. Later that evening, I rubbed Noxzema Skin Cream on her sunburned shoulders. That, I think, is when I discovered I was in love, and to this day Noxzema Skin Cream smells like love to me.

Only now, these many years later, do I realize that the source of my joy that sunlit afternoon was not young love, but God. He was the One who brought us together, who made our running laughter a kind of holy music, who destined that we would one day marry and give birth to a child of our own.

In truth, once we understand that every experience is infused with His presence, all of life becomes a sanctuary and each experience, no matter how mundane, an opportunity to encounter Him. The beauty of nature, the birth of a child, the majesty of a great piece of music, a wedding, a special book or movie, even the death of a friend or family member all become opportunities for Him to reveal Himself to us.

Another time I experienced His nearness while Brenda and I were eating fried chicken from a fast-food place, sitting cross-legged on the floor of the living room, with our backs against a roll of carpet. Although we were physically tired, our weariness was infused with a sense of accomplishment. For the better part of three weeks, we had poured ourselves into that run-down rent house, and it was finally starting to feel like home.

Swallowing one last bite of chicken, I leaned back against the roll of carpet and wiped my hands on my soiled jeans. Looking at Brenda, I thought how blessed I am. At eighteen she had committed her life to me, for better or for worse, holding nothing back. Without a complaint she had accompanied me to one struggling church after another. She was my closest friend, my lover, and the mother of our daughter.

That afternoon, she was wearing jeans and a T-shirt. Her hair was a mess, and there was a smudge of paint on her cheek. Still, she had never looked better, and I loved her more than I can say.

The sound of children's laughter drifted in through the open window, in the distance a dog barked, and belatedly I realized that God was with us. I'm not sure where that thought came from, but suddenly it was there, full-blown and as clear as any thought I've ever had. In a strange sort of way, that unfinished living room became a sanctuary—

chicken and corn-on-the-cob a holy meal, and our conversation a kind of prayer.

Now before you decide I've lost my mind or committed a sacrilege, take a minute and remember how often God revealed Himself to ordinary people in the most ordinary ways. The best known of course is the incarnation—God incognito!—"The Word became flesh and lived among us...."[129]

To the busy innkeeper, Jesus was just another baby. To Peter and his fishing buddies, He was just a beachcomber squatting beside a breakfast fire in the early morning mist. Only later, after He called to them, did they recognize Him as the Lord. To the two despairing disciples on the road to Emmaus, He was just a stranger, and an unusually uniformed one at that. He spent an entire day in their company before they realized who He was.

What am I trying to say? Just this: "Listen to your life. See it for the fathomless mystery it is. In the boredom and pain of it no less than in the excitement and gladness touch, taste, smell your way to the holy and hidden heart of it because in the last analysis all moments are key moments, and life itself is grace."[130]

Do that, and like the two disciples on the road to Emmaus, you will discover that Christ is near even when you are sure He is nowhere to be found. And in finding Him, you will discover your faith and your reason for living.

CHAPTER ELEVEN

Saul of Tarsus

Acts 9:1-19; 22:1-16

AFTER SIX LONG DAYS ON THE road, we are finally nearing Damascus, and not any too soon as far as I am concerned. The heat, the dust, and the boredom have rubbed my emotions raw, not to mention the magnitude of my assignment, which never ceases to weigh on my mind. In my bag, I carry letters from the high priest in Jerusalem, authorizing me to arrest and extradite those followers of the Way who have fled to Damascus in hopes of escaping the purge. But they will not escape, for we are committed to ridding Israel of this divisive and blasphemous sect at any cost. They will be imprisoned, beaten, even put to death if necessary.

Although I am a Hebrew of the Hebrews, I was not reared in Jerusalem or even in Palestine. I was born in Tarsus, the capital of the province of Cilicia, in the southeast of Asia Minor. Being the son of a merchant, expectations regarding my future were limited. Most people thought I would follow in my father's steps, but at an early age my intellectual gifts became apparent. Even my father, who longed for a son to take over the family business, recognized that a career in commerce would be a terrible waste. At the age of thirteen, my scholarship afforded me the opportunity to study in Jerusalem with Gamaliel, the greatest of all Jewish rabbis.

Having recently been accepted as a full-fledged member of the Sanhedrin, I have achieved far more than might be expected of someone from my background. And this commission to persecute the followers of the Way proves how highly I am thought of, yet I don't feel the way I expected to feel. For all my achievements, I feel like something is missing or that I am missing something.

Pushing such thoughts from my mind, I focus on the task ahead. It is holy work and something to be proud of, so why do I feel ashamed? These false teachers, who would make a god out of a dead man, have brought judgment on themselves. They have turned away from the one true God and are trying to persuade others to do the same. The Torah makes our duty clear:

> "If your very own brother, or your son or daughter, or the wife you love, or your closest friend secretly entices you, saying, 'Let us go and worship other gods' (gods that neither you nor your fathers have known, gods of the peoples around you, whether near or far, from one end

of the land to the other), do not yield to him or listen to him. Show him no pity. Do not spare him or shield him. You must certainly put him to death. Your hand must be the first in putting him to death, and then the hands of all the people. Stone him to death, because he tried to turn you away from the LORD your God, who brought you out of Egypt, out of the land of slavery. You must purge the evil from among you."[131]

What I am doing is God's work, of that I am sure; at least that is what I tell myself. The evil of this false teaching must be purged from among us and those who teach it as well. I will show them no mercy. Let their blood be upon their own heads.

Even as I strengthen myself for the task ahead, I am assailed by a memory I cannot excise, no matter how hard I try, nor the questions it raises. Why would a scholar, well steeped in the Torah, claim a dead carpenter from Nazareth was the Messiah? Why am I so discomfited by his arguments and the evidence he presented? Why am I haunted by the possibility that this Jesus, whom we had crucified, might truly be the Christ?

If I am honest with myself, I will have to admit that we could not refute Stephen's arguments. His grasp of the

Torah and his insight into the Holy Scriptures was remarkable and for a time he held the entire Sanhedrin spellbound. But our minds were made up and when reason failed we turned to rage. In an instant we became a mob intent on mayhem and death. Although I screamed as loudly as the rest, I could not bring myself to hurl a single stone. I consented to his death, but I could not bring myself to participate in the actual stoning.

Noticing my reticence, some of the more fanatical members of the Sanhedrin suggested I might be a sympathizer or even a secret disciple. Their accusations infuriated me and caused me no little concern. Realizing their suspicions might well undermine my career aspirations, I set out to prove my zeal. I became the most passionate persecutor of those who followed the Way. Going from house to house, I dragged men and women off and put them in prison.

Among the Sanhedrin, my reputation as a zealot grew and when someone was needed to lead an organized effort to rid Israel of these blasphemers, I was selected. The appointment strengthened my position, and I set about my task with a fanatical zeal. Such work is not without its risks, however, and I soon found myself sleeping poorly, or not at all. Most troubling was my growing fear that I might be on the wrong side of this issue. Of course, I couldn't discuss my concerns with any of my colleagues, so I was left to fend for myself.

Of particular concern was the way Stephen died. The more the Sanhedrin had raged the calmer he became. While we were gnashing our teeth and screaming at him, the most peaceful expression came over his face. Looking up, as if he could see into Heaven, he said, "Look. The heavens are open and I see the Son of Man standing at the right hand of God."[132]

We might have let him off with a beating had he not said that, but with those words he sealed his fate. Covering our ears and screaming, we rushed at him and dragged him to a steep hill just outside the city. Shoving him into a deep ravine, we rained stones down upon him. In short order he was driven to his knees, his head and face a bloody mess.

I had turned away, having no stomach for the grisly end, when I heard him cry out, "Lord, do not hold my blood against them."[133] Turning back, I watched as he died beneath a final barrage of stones.

When I can't sleep at night, I find myself asking what kind of a man prays for his executioners. A better man than me, I can tell you that. More importantly, why would an intelligent man like the scholar be willing to die to perpetuate a hoax?

There's only one answer—he wouldn't!

Jesus may not be who He claimed to be, but I am convinced that Stephen believed He was the Christ. There is no other explanation for his devotion or for the fanatical devotion of these followers of the Way. They are willing not only to suffer imprisonment, but to die rather than renounce their faith. That they truly believe this Jesus is the Messiah is obvious, and it's enough to cause a reasonable man no little concern.

My ruminating is cut short by a blinding flash of light that knocks me to my knees. And out of the light there comes a Voice roaring in my ears, calling me by name and demanding to know why I am persecuting Him to death. Nearly tongued-tied with fear I manage to croak, "Who are You, Lord?"

"I am Jesus the Christ, the One you are persecuting."

My worst fear has been realized. In my zeal I have been fighting God himself. In pursuing the followers of the Way, I have been persecuting the Messiah. Inasmuch as I have done injustice to the very least of His brethren, I have done injustice to Him. Their blood is upon my hands.

Pressing my face to the ground, I wait for His wrath to fall, knowing no man ever deserved it more.

"On your feet," He commands. "Go into the city and wait. You will be told what you must do."

Although I am weak with fear, I manage to stagger to my feet, but I can't see. Balling up my fists, I knead my eyes but to no avail. My eyes are open but I can't see, not even my hand in front of my face.

Above the persistent ringing in my ears, I hear the voices of my companions. They are hurling questions at one another, but no one seems to know what happened.

"Help me," I call to them. "I am blind. I can't see a thing."

In my zeal I have been fighting God himself.

Their confused jabbering stumbles to a stop. Finally, one of them takes me by the hand and leads me to a small donkey. After rearranging the bundles they help me mount.

"Take me to the house of Jude on Straight Street. He is expecting us."

For three days and three nights, I take neither food nor water. My world has been turned upside down and I have no appetite. In the darkness, I am tormented by the memories of what I have done. Blind though I am, I still see the faces of those I have tortured and imprisoned. Nor can I quiet the grief-stricken wails of the children whose parents I have taken from them. How grotesque my earlier fanaticism now seems. I must have been a mad man to have thought I could serve God by torture and mayhem.

Unanswered questions buzz inside my head like angry hornets. Am I going to be blind for the rest of my life? Is this darkness the judgment of God? Am I being punished for my arrogance and pride? Will I be tortured as I have tortured the followers of the Way? Around and around the questions go, but I have no answers.

When my despair reaches its most debilitating point, when I am sure there is no hope for me, either in this life or the next, the most amazing thing happens. I am given a vision, and in this vision I see a man placing his hands upon my eyes and restoring my sight. Although I am sure I have never seen him, I know who he is. Ananias is his name. How I know that I cannot tell you. I just know.

The meaning of the vision is unclear, but it has given me a breath of hope. Perhaps this Ananias is a messenger sent by God not only to restore my sight, but to heal my soul. Maybe I am going to be given a second chance, a chance to atone for the evil I have done. As unlikely as that seems, it has given me a fragile hope, and I desperately cling to it.

On the fourth day, I have a visitor, Ananias—the man I saw in the vision. Placing his hands on my eyes he says, "Saul, you are now our brother. I have been sent to you by the Lord Jesus—the same Lord who appeared to you on the

The meaning of the vision is unclear, but it has given me a breath of hope.

road as you were coming here. He sent me so you might see again and be filled with the Holy Spirit."

At his words my heart leaps within me and when he removes his hands, a scaly film falls from my eyes and I can see. Leaping to my feet, I began to praise the Lord.

After a bit I regain my composure and Ananias begins to prophesy, "Saul, you have been chosen by the God of our fathers to know His will and to see the Righteous One and to hear words from His mouth. You will be His witness to all men of what you have seen and heard."

Can this be? Can I, a blasphemer, a persecutor of the church, a murderer of believers, now be a witness for Him? Is there no limit to His forgiveness, no sinner He cannot restore?

While I am still pondering his words he says, "What are you waiting for? Get up and be baptized. Wash your sins away and call on His name."

Turning on his heel, Ananias heads for the back of the house. Scrambling to my feet, I hurry after him. In the garden behind the house, Jude has a fountain and a small pool to which we make our way. Wading into the pool Ananias motions for me to follow him. As I move into the water, the significance of what I am about to do hits me with a force that nearly takes my breath away. By following the Lord Jesus in baptism, I am renouncing my old life in its entirety. I will be misunderstood by my family, rejected by my peers, and ostracized by the Sanhedrin. If I do this, I will be turning my back on everything I have worked so hard to achieve.

Ananias reaches for me and I give him my hand, allowing him to lead me into the center of the small pool. "Saul of Tarsus," he says, looking me in the eye, "I now baptize you in the name of the Lord Jesus Christ."

Without hesitation, he plunges me completely beneath the water, burying my old life with its sins. When I emerge from the water, it is as if I have been born again. All the guilt and condemnation are gone. In their place, I have an overwhelming peace. Lifting my hands into the air I shout, "Jesus Christ is my Lord!"

> If I do this, I will be turning my back on everything I have worked so hard to achieve.

ENCOUNTERS WITH CHRIST 213

The next few days are a blur. I spend considerable time with the disciples in Damascus, who, at first, regard me with no little fear. Who can blame them, considering the havoc I have wrought. Many have family members in prison, put there by my fanatical zeal. Still, once they realize my conversion is sincere, they receive me with an outpouring of love.

Being a devout observer of the Law and highly respected by all the Jews in Damascus, Ananias offers to accompany me to the synagogue. I am grateful, for his testimony will corroborate my witness. Of course, if the religious leaders here are anything like their counterparts in Jerusalem, they will be immune to reason.

At the synagogue we are received respectfully. The religious leaders know who I am and why I have come. That is, they know that I have been sent from the high priest to rid them of the troublesome followers of the Way. What they have no way of knowing is that I am now one of them. Jesus is my Messiah, and I believe that God has raised Him from the dead.

As I recount all that has happened to me since that blinding flash of light knocked me to the ground as I was approaching Damascus, the religious leaders are dumbfounded. They whisper among themselves, questioning one another. "Isn't this the man who raised havoc in Jerusalem? Didn't he go from house to house, dragging off men and women, putting them into prison? Wasn't he sent here by the chief priest to arrest and extradite the followers of the Way? What has happened to him? Is he mad?"

Although they question me at length, I can see they do not believe. Nor are they open to the truth of the Scriptures. Beginning with Moses and the prophets, I use their own Scriptures to show them that Jesus is truly the promised Messiah; still they refuse to believe. Though they are powerless to refute the truth of Scripture, still they harden their hearts. Well it has been said, "No man is so blind as he who will not see."

Like the Sanhedrin before them, they decide that if they cannot refute the message they will kill the messenger. Word

What they have no way of knowing is that I am now one of them.

of their decision reaches the ears of Ananias and before they can seize me, he arranges for me to go into hiding. Being a man of action, the inactivity nearly drives me mad. The tension is unbearable. Every time a voice is heard in the street or a knock comes on the door, I brace myself.

After several days I can bear no more and I insist that we find a way for me to escape the city. Ananias and some of the others try to talk me out of it, but I will not be put off. Finally, someone hits upon a plan to lower me over the city wall in a basket, seeing that the Jews are closely watching the city gates both day and night.

Under the cover of darkness, we make our way to an opening high in the wall that surrounds the city. After embracing each other, I climb into the basket and they begin lowering me to the ground. The basket bumps and scrapes against the wall. Although it is just a little noise, in my ears it sounds loud enough to wake the dead. I hold my breath waiting for someone to sound the alarm, but nothing happens. At last the basket bumps against the ground. Hurriedly, I climb out and give the rope a hard tug.

Standing in the darkness cast by the shadow of that imposing wall, I hear again the words of Ananias, "You are God's chosen instrument to carry the name of Jesus to the

Gentiles and their kings, and to the people of Israel as well. God will show you how much you must suffer for His name."

Breathing a silent prayer, I step out of the shadows and set off on the journey that will ultimately cost me my life. I don't know what's going to happen, but I do know that the Holy Spirit has told me that I will face hardships and prison. Be that as it may, I consider my life worth nothing to me, if only I may finish the race and complete the task the Lord Jesus has given me—the task of taking the gospel of God's grace to the Gentiles.[134]

Life Lessons

LIFE LESSONS

Saul of Tarsus

IN THE HISTORY OF THE Christian church, there is no conversion more momentous than that of Saul of Tarsus. Even before his conversion, God was directing his steps in order to prepare him for his unique destiny. Saul, who later changed his name to Paul,[135] had a varied background that uniquely prepared him for his ministry. Being born and raised in Tarsus during the Roman occupation meant he was a Roman citizen, which gave him a distinct advantage in his missionary travels. His early years in Tarsus gave him a familiarity with Greek culture and the Roman world, enabling him to speak to different people at many different levels. "Paul was his Latin or Roman name, Saul his Jewish name; Greek culture was his conditioning, Hebraism his training, and life in Christ his purpose and passion. A man for all nations and all seasons."[136]

While each and every conversion is a miracle of God's grace,[137] Saul's conversion demonstrates God's unconditional love and limitless mercy in a way few others can. Writing of his conversion he says, "Even though I was once a blasphemer and a persecutor and a violent man, I was shown mercy because I acted in ignorance and unbelief. The grace of our Lord was poured out on me abundantly, along with the faith and love that are in Christ Jesus. Here is a trustworthy saying that deserves full acceptance: Christ Jesus came into the world to save sinners—of whom I am the worst. But for that very reason I was shown mercy so that in me, the worst of sinners, Christ Jesus might display his unlimited patience as an example for those who would believe on him and receive eternal life."[138]

While there are many facets of his life and ministry that are of interest, I would like to focus on his conversion. He was not seeking Christ; in fact, his only interest in Him revolved around persecuting and imprisoning those who were His followers. Even at that critical moment when he encountered Christ on the road to Damascus, he was on his way to arrest and extradite those Jewish believers who had fled from Jerusalem. This single event, perhaps more than any other, demonstrates to what extremes God will go in order to reconcile us to Himself.

And it is not just those individuals who, like Saul, are destined for special service in the kingdom who are the recipients of God's extravagant pursuit. Let me illustrate. As a young man of twenty-one, I was serving my first church, a small congregation in the farming community of Holly, Colorado. In pursuit of my pastoral duties, I often went to Lil's Cafe to fellowship with the local businessmen during their mid-morning coffee break. One of the regulars was the local crop duster—a hard-drinking man and a womanizer, who was estranged from his third wife.

His name was Bob, and unbeknown to me, he bet several of the businessmen that he could make the preacher cuss. If he could make me swear in their presence, they had to pay him $50—a tidy sum in those days. Failing to make me cuss, he had to attend the next Sunday service at the church where I served as pastor.

Of course, Bob lost that wager and the next Sunday evening he joined us for worship. In those days our Sunday evening attendance usually numbered less than a dozen, meaning Bob stuck out like a sore thumb.

At the conclusion of my sermon, I invited the congregation to join me at the front of the church to receive Holy Communion. Since we had a guest present, I was careful to explain that our congregation practiced open communion and that you did not have to be a member of our local fellowship to share the Lord's Supper with us.

Not wanting to appear unchurched, Bob joined the rest of the congregation when they came forward to receive the emblems. When I served him, I made it a point to tell him that the apostle Paul warned us that if anyone partook of the bread or the cup of the Lord in an unworthy manner that he was eating and drinking judgment on himself.[139] After the benediction, I couldn't help but notice that Bob had left the communion elements untouched, on the altar where he had been kneeling.

On Tuesday evening, Brenda and I were watching television in the parsonage, which was located next door to the church. Sometime around seven o'clock, I began to feel like I should go to the church. It made no sense, so I tried to ignore it. When the feeling persisted for at least thirty minutes, I decided to head for the church. If nothing else, I could spend some time praying in the empty sanctuary.

As I descended the steps and turned toward the church, Bob's pickup slid around the corner and skidded to a stop. Leaping out, he hurried to the front door of the church and started jerking on the door handle. Once I got the door unlocked, he pushed by me and ran to the altar where he fell on his knees.

For the next fifteen or twenty minutes, he wept before the Lord, confessing his sins and calling on the name of Jesus. When he finally finished, he looked up and gave me a joyous smile. Noticing the communion service sitting on the table behind me he asked, "May I receive Holy Communion now?"

Without a moment's hesitation, I selected the elements and knelt down beside him. Breaking the bread I said, "On the night Jesus was betrayed He took bread and broke it and blessed it saying, 'Take, eat, this is my body which is broken for you.'"[140] Together, Bob and I partook of the bread.

Holding the cup I said, "In the same manner, Jesus took the cup saying, 'This is my blood of the new testament which is shed for the remission of your sins. Drink ye all of it.'" Together, we lifted our cups and partook.

Later, Bob shared the details leading up to his remarkable conversion. For two days the Holy Spirit had been dealing with his heart, ever more intensely. Finally, while he was eating dinner at Lil's Cafe, the Spirit of the Lord came upon him in such a powerful way that he felt that if he didn't give his life to Jesus that very moment he might well be lost for all eternity. Throwing some money on the table, he rushed from the cafe and drove directly to the church.

That was more than thirty-seven years ago, and Bob has never been the same. He now serves Jesus with the same kind of uninhibited passion that once characterized his life of sin.

When I think of Saul of Tarsus, I see a resourceful scholar and a natural leader. Born and raised by Hebrew parents in Hellenistic Tarsus, he had both Hebrew tradition and Greek culture flowing in his nature. He was both a Hebrew Pharisee and a man of the world. Being fluent in Greek, Hebrew, and Aramaic, he was exactly the kind of man Jesus needed to lead His infant Church. Without him, or someone like him, the New Testament Church would not have grown into the spiritual force that changed the world.[141] Little wonder that the Lord pursued him until He caught him on the road just outside of Damascus. Forgiven and transformed, he became the Church's foremost apostle and the author of much of the New Testament.

When I think of Bob, I see a blue-collar worker with a limited education. Other than being able to fly a crop dusting plane with remarkable skill, he had no obvious gifts. Relationally he was handicapped. Try as he might he could not make a success of marriage. At the time of his conversion, he was estranged from his third wife. Hardly the kind of man you would expect the Lord to go after, but He did! He pursued him until He caught him in Lil's Cafe, near Highway 50 in Southeastern Colorado.

Saul of Tarsus and Bob the crop duster—unlike in every way except for their need of a Savior. Unlike in every way except for the grace of God that would not give up on them. Unlike in every way except their sins have been forgiven and their names have been written in the Lamb's Book of Life. Unlike in every way except they both call Jesus Lord and serve Him passionately. Unlike in every way except they are both fellow citizens with God's people and members of God's household.

CHAPTER TWELVE

John the Apostle

Revelation 1:9-18

SEEKING SOLITUDE, I PUSH MY weary body up the steep path. When my breathing becomes labored, I pause, listening to the pounding of the surf as it beats itself into a foamy spray against the jagged rocks, hundreds of feet below. It is a welcome relief from the clanging of chisels on rock and the grunts and cursing of weary men at hard labor. For the most part, my fellow prisoners are common criminals, troublemakers, who have been exiled to the rock quarries on this small island. Though I try to befriend them, the truth is, we have little in common.

Shading my eyes I can just make out the hazy outline of the coast of Asia Minor. Although distance does not permit me to see it, I know that the city of Ephesus is situated at a port along the coast. Thinking of that dying city, I cannot help but wonder how the brothers and sisters are doing. I pray they do not lose heart. They have suffered much for the gospel, and they took it hard when Domitian,

Emperor of Rome, banished me to the Isle of Patmos for refusing to renounce Christ.

I am an old man now and more than a little homesick. Not for Capernaum, though there are times that I remember my youth with nostalgia, especially the time I spent upon the water with James and my father. No, I am homesick for Heaven and those who await me there. Of the original apostles, I am the only one still living. They died violent deaths, all of them—crucified, beheaded, beaten to death. Tragic though their deaths were, the shedding of their blood only served to advance the cause of Christ. Praise be to His Holy name.

Having caught my breath, I resume my climb but at a slower pace. It is the Lord's Day and I am looking for a place out of the sun where I can worship without interruption. Being a penal colony, privacy is at a premium on this tiny island, still I find what I am looking for—a shaded place beneath an outcropping of rock. Lowering myself to the ground, I arrange my back against the rock wall and reach for my water bag. Tipping it up, I drink deeply.

When I have quenched my thirst, I place the water bag on the ground beside me. Closing my eyes, I let my mind wander. Like a river rushing to the sea, my thoughts inevitably return to my early days with Jesus. I could never forget the miracles—the turning of water into wine in Cana of Galilee,[142] the healing of the man born blind,[143] or how the woman with an incurable issue of blood was restored just by touching his clothes.[144] And who could ever forget the raising of the widow's son[145] or the glorious transfiguration of the Lord himself?[146] Still, when I think of those early years, it is the relationships that I remember, the camaraderie we shared with each other, but especially with Jesus.

The record of our Lord's earthly ministry has been well documented. With the help of John Mark, Peter recorded a brief history, as did Matthew and Luke. Of course, I wrote my own account which is somewhat different from theirs. It is not contradictory, it is simply written from a different perspective. While theirs focused on the events, I tried to focus on the relationships. Taken together, they provide an accurate, if incomplete, account. The fact is, Jesus did many other things as well. If every one of them were written down, I suppose that even the whole world would not have room for the books that would be written.[147]

It is to those things that my thoughts return at times like this. To the things we didn't record—not because they were not important for they were, but because they were so personal, so private. In his public ministry, we saw the Christ—the glory of the Word made flesh and dwelling among us. The glory of the One and Only, who came from the Father, full of grace and truth.[148] In those private moments we saw Jesus, Mary's son. You might think that would make it harder for us to believe He was the Son of God, but it didn't.

Sometimes these two sides of Jesus' nature were so apparent that even the most dim-witted disciple couldn't miss it. For instance, as a man He often became physically exhausted. Once He was so tired that He slept through a life-threatening storm, yet as the divine Son of God, He commanded the winds and waves to cease, and they obeyed Him.[149] As a man, He was so deeply grieved by the death of His friend Lazarus that He wept. As the Son of God, He raised Lazarus from the dead.[150] Of course, nowhere is this more clearly seen than in His own death and resurrection. As a man, He died on the cross and was buried. As the Son of God, He conquered death, hell, and the grave!

Jesus was the most selfless person I have ever known. Not once did He use His divine power for His own benefit. For instance, He refused to turn stones into bread to satisfy His own hunger, yet He multiplied the bread and fish in order to feed the five thousand. He never hesitated to use His divine power to help others, but no matter how exhausted He might be, He never used it to rejuvenate himself.

Well do I remember the night He washed our feet. Some of the disciples thought I should be the one to do it since I was the youngest, but I adamantly refused, as did we all. Finally, Jesus laid aside His outer garments and gird himself with a towel. Taking a basin of water, He began to wash our feet. Though He might have rebuked us, He did not. Instead, He simply said, "If I, your Lord and Teacher, have washed your feet, you also should wash one another's feet."[151]

His gracious act of love shamed me. How petty my pride seemed in light of His humble service. Silently I vowed that I would commit my life in loving service to Him and to others. How clear it had all been in that moment, how simple.

How petty my pride seemed in light of His humble service.

Whoever loves God must also love his brother.[152] Not with mere words either, but with action and in truth.[153]

Thinking about these things now, I lift my hands in worship. "Praise be to Jesus Christ who is the faithful witness, the firstborn from the dead, and the ruler of the kings of the earth. Praise be to Him who loves us and has freed us from our sins by His blood, and has made us to be kings and priests to serve His God and Father—to Him be glory and power for ever and ever! Amen."

I lose myself in the Spirit as I pour out my love for my Savior and my King. In His presence the difficulties of my present state seem almost inconsequential. Of what concern are my sufferings when compared with the glories to come? He has promised never to forsake me and as long as He is near, I will gladly suffer anything. More precious to me is He than family or friends or any earthly thing.

Suddenly my reverie is shattered by what at first sounds like the blast of a trumpet. But it is not a trumpet, it is a voice. A voice so rich and resonate that I can only liken it to a musical instrument. Its clear timbre surrounds me, washes over me like the pealing of a bell. Although I have never heard anything like it, it is familiar in a way I cannot explain and I find myself embracing it.

Getting to my feet, I look around, searching for the One whose voice I hear. The familiar trail with its outcropping of volcanic rock is gone, and in its place I see seven golden lampstands. Standing among the lampstands is someone I can only liken to Daniel's "Son of Man."[154] So overpowering is His presence that I fall at His feet like a dead man. Even though I can hardly breathe, my eyes are drawn to Him.

That the One who speaks with me is Jesus, I have no doubt, yet His glory is unlike anything I have ever seen. He is magnificent beyond description. I was with Jesus on the mount when He was transfigured before us and we beheld His radiant glory,[155] but it could not compare to this. When He ascended into heaven,[156] I was there. I witnessed that glorious event, I saw the angels and heard them speaking, but it was nothing like this.

He is dressed in a robe reaching down to His feet and with a golden sash around

His glory is unlike anything I have ever seen. He is magnificent beyond description.

His chest. His head and hair are white like wool, as white as snow, and His eyes are like blazing fire. His feet are like bronze glowing in a furnace, and His voice is like the sound of rushing waters. In His right hand He holds seven stars, and out of His mouth comes a sharp double-edged sword. His face is like the sun shining in all its brilliance.

In the presence of such transcendent glory, I am acutely aware of my own insignificance and I hear myself crying, "O Lord, What is man that You are mindful of him, the son of man that You care for him?" Never, never have I felt so small, so unimportant; yet, as paradoxical as it may seem, I have never felt more valued, more loved.

Suddenly I am caught up in the Spirit and transported into the very throne room of Heaven. I see things so glorious I cannot possibly describe them. Encircling the throne are four living creatures, twenty-four elders, and a great host of angels numbering thousands upon thousands, and ten thousand times ten thousand. They are singing, and the sound of their worship fills all there is:

> "Worthy is the Lamb, who was slain,
> to receive power and wealth and
> wisdom and strength
> and honor and glory and praise!"[157]

And then they are joined in heavenly song by every creature in Heaven and on Earth and under the Earth and on the sea. As one they lift their voices in praise to the Lamb:

> "To him who sits on the throne and
>   to the Lamb
> be praise and honor and glory and power,
>   for ever and ever!"[158]

When at last the anthem reaches its crescendo, the four living creatures shout, "Amen," and the four and twenty elders fall prostrate before the throne in worship. Although I am just a witness to these things, I, too, fall to my knees and press my face to the ground.

How long I am caught up in the Spirit I do not know, but suddenly the scene changes. Now I see things that are to come. There is war in the heavens and on Earth, great tribulation such as there has never been since the beginning of time. Temporarily the sun, the moon, and the stars lose a portion of their light and the earth is plunged into an ice age. There are violent storms and catastrophic earthquakes. Famine is widespread and incurable diseases kill hundreds of millions. If those days had not been cut short, no one could have survived.

After this I looked and there before me was a great multitude that no one could count, from every nation, tribe, people, and language, standing before the throne and in front of the Lamb. They were wearing white robes and were holding palm branches in their hands. And they cried out in a loud voice:

> "Salvation belongs to our God,
> who sits on the throne,
> and to the Lamb."[159]

Then one of the elders said, "These are they who have come out of the great tribulation; they have washed their robes and made them white in the blood of the Lamb. Therefore,

> they are before the throne of God
> and serve him day and night in his temple;
> and he who sits on the throne will spread his tent
>   over them.
> Never again will they hunger;
> never again will they thirst.
> The sun will not beat upon them,

nor any scorching heat.
For the Lamb at the center of the throne will be
their shepherd;
he will lead them to springs of living water.
And God will wipe away every tear from their
eyes."[160]

Just as suddenly as the vision began it is over, and I am back on the Isle of Patmos. My water bag is lying in the dust where I left it, and the steep path looks the same as it always has. But things are not the same, for He is standing before me. Reaching down He places His right hand on me, and a familiar touch it is. "Do not be afraid," He says. "I am the First and the Last. I am the Living One; I was dead, and behold I am alive for ever and ever! And I hold the keys of death and Hades."

And then He is gone and I am alone on this lonely outcropping of volcanic rock. For all I have experienced, I am still a prisoner of Rome and tomorrow I will return to the rock quarries, where I will work alongside the other exiles. Yet, in another sense I will never be the same again. For I have seen the future and the future is God!

Empires will rise and fall. Kings will come and go, but He will reign forever. Then the end will come, when he hands over the kingdom to God the Father after he has destroyed all dominion, authority, and power. For he must reign until he has put all his enemies under his feet. The last enemy to be destroyed is death...When he has done this, then the Son himself will be made subject to him who put everything under him, so that God may be all in all.[161]

Life Lessons

LIFE LESSONS
John the Apostle

AMONG THE MANY THINGS JOHN'S encounter with Christ on the Isle of Patmos teaches us is that the best of things can come out of the worst of situations. Being exiled to work in a rock quarry among hardened criminals is just about as bad as it gets, especially if you are an old man nearing the end of your life. Having a visitation from the glorified Son of God and being given the Revelation of things to come is just about as good as it gets. I am not suggesting that God arranged for John to be exiled to Patmos, but He certainly redeemed it. If John had to be alone on that barren island, then the Lord would use his isolation as an opportunity to give him, and ultimately the Church, the revelation that composes the final book in Holy Canon. Of all the contributions John made to the kingdom, that may be his greatest.

Years ago, I heard a wonderful Bible teacher say that God allows things to happen to us, so He can do something in us, in order to do something through us. We see this principle at work again and again in the lives of the patriarchs, prophets, and apostles. Jealousy sent Joseph to slavery in

Egypt,[162] vindictiveness put him in prison,[163] but God used it all to position him as the second most powerful man in Egypt.[164] An evil edict forced Moses' parents to place him in a tiny papyrus basket in the Nile in an attempt to save his life.[165] God used that situation to awaken compassion in the heart of Pharaoh's daughter, who adopted Moses, rearing him in the palace where he was educated and prepared for his life mission.[166] Persecution imprisoned the apostle Paul, effectively curtailing his ministry as a missionary. God used that "down" time to inspire Paul to write much of the New Testament. Of his prison experiences Paul wrote, "Now I want you to know, brothers, that what has happened to me has really served to advance the gospel."[167]

When you find yourself in a difficult place, resist the temptation to ask why. Instead, ask how. Not why did this happen to me, but how is God going to use this? Instead of resenting the unfairness of life and fighting against your circumstances, make peace with them. If you give God a chance, He will use the worst life can do to make you the best you can be. Remember, "...he who began a good work in you will carry it on to completion until the day of Christ Jesus."[168]

Another thing we learn from John is not to fear. When Jesus came to him on the Isle of Patmos, He said, "Do not be afraid."[169]

It was a timely word for John, and it is a timely word for those of us living in the twenty-first century. Faced with what is happening in our world—sexual predators preying on our children, serial killers stalking our streets, suicide bombers killing without conscience, terrorists jockeying for weapons of mass destruction—it is easy to be anxious, even fearful.

As I write this, authorities in Aruba are searching for clues as to what happened in the disappearance of eighteen-year-old Natalee Holloway, a recent high school graduate, who disappeared while on a five-day senior trip with classmates. In Fresno, California, a jury decides on the death penalty for Marcus Wesson, who was convicted on nine counts of first degree murder. All of the victims—ages one to twenty-five—were his children, some of whom were fathered with his own daughters and nieces. In Kabul, Afghanistan, the United States military recovers the bodies of sixteen soldiers, who were killed when the Chinook helicopter that was transporting them was shot down by a rocket-propelled grenade fired by Taliban fighters. And that is just a small sampling of the kinds of things that are happening in our world on a daily basis.

On a front closer to home for many of us, economic downsizing and outsourcing make job security a thing of the past, and the ongoing Social Security crisis, not to mention pension debacles, makes retirement iffy. The escalating health care crisis threatens the well-being of young and old alike. New antibiotic-resistant strains of bacteria-producing disease threaten to launch a worldwide epidemic, not to mention the ever increasing threat of a terrorist attack utilizing biological weapons. No wonder Jesus said that men would faint from terror, apprehensive of what was happening in the world.[170]

There's more, but I think you probably get the point. The world into which I was born—I'm fifty-eight—is gone, replaced by an ever changing and ever more dangerous one. I'm not so concerned about myself, but I cannot help but wonder what kind of world my grandchildren will grow up in.

When I am tempted to be afraid, or even anxious, I remind myself that Jesus said He would never leave us or forsake us.[171] "So we say with confidence, 'The Lord is my helper; I will not be afraid. What can man do to me?'"[172]

No matter what you are facing, no matter how dark and foreboding the future seems, you can be assured that God sees your situation. He cares what happens to you, He hears your desperate prayers, even those you can't articulate, and He will help you. You can count on that![173]

The definitive life lesson John's experience affords us is the assurance that Jesus will ultimately triumph, His kingdom is coming! One day the kingdoms of this world will "become the kingdom of our Lord and of His Christ, and He will reign for ever and ever."[174]

From a purely human perspective, such a thing must have been nearly incomprehensible for the first century believers. Rome was the ultimate power and they were the disenfranchised, the persecuted. Roman might had turned Christian baptism into a blood bath. All of the apostles, save one, had been martyred, along with tens of thousands of others. Even John, at the time he received this word, was a prisoner of Rome, an exile doing hard labor in a rock quarry on Patmos.

Still, it is well to remember that what we can see is temporary, but what is unseen in the Spirit world is eternal.[175] Twenty centuries later the Roman Empire is ancient history. The Coliseum, where Christians were put to death for sport, is nothing more than a tourist attraction, while the Church of Jesus Christ is marching toward that climactic moment when all nations will come and worship the Lord.[176]

In the 1970's, a minister "prophesied" that the Soviet Union would collapse and that following its collapse, there would be a great spiritual awaking in Eastern Europe and the former Soviet block countries. I managed not to snicker when I heard about it, but just barely. I told someone that it was a good thing we didn't stone false prophets or that man would surely die.

As far as I was concerned, there was no way his prophecy was going to come true. The Soviet Union was a super power, an atheistic government that persecuted Christians, and the possibility of its demise was inconceivable to me. I should have reread Daniel, especially that part about a rock that is not made by human hands. Daniel put it like this: "the God of heaven will set up a kingdom that will never be destroyed, nor will it be left to another people. It will crush all those kingdoms and bring them to an end, but it will itself endure forever. This is the meaning of the vision of the rock cut out of a mountain, but not by human hands."[177]

At this point, I pause in my writing to glance at the wall to my left. Prominently displayed among my memorabilia is a piece of the Berlin Wall, or perhaps I should say what used to be the Berlin Wall, for on November 9, 1989, that wall came down. Following that historic moment, Communist governments began to fall in rapid succession. Finally, the Soviet Union itself collapsed in August 1991.

What neither military might nor the threat of nuclear war could do, God did! And there followed a spiritual awakening in the former Soviet Union of nearly unprecedented magnitude. Old churches were reopened, new churches were planted, and Bibles were freely distributed in schools and hospitals. High ranking government officials made public confessions of their new faith in Christ. God's kingdom was coming!

No matter how grim the world situation looks at this present time we can rest in the certain knowledge that the kingdom of God will ultimately triumph. Good will overcome evil. Truth will triumph. Righteousness will displace unrighteousness and love will conquer all. That's the glorious revelation that John was given on the Isle of Patmos, under the worst of circumstances.

"And I heard a loud voice from the throne saying, 'Now the dwelling of God is with men, and he will live with them. They will be his people, and God himself will be with them and be their God. He will wipe every tear from their eyes. There will be no more death or mourning or crying or pain, for the old order of things has passed away.'"[178]

And so we pray, "Come Lord Jesus. Establish Your Kingdom in us and on Earth. May Your will be done on Earth as it is in Heaven. For Yours is the kingdom and the power and the glory for ever. Amen."

ABOUT THE AUTHOR

Richard Exley is a passionate person who cares deeply for people. His devotion is reflected in all his endeavors. He is a man with a rich diversity of experience as a pastor, counselor, radio host, conference and retreat speaker, as well as a best-selling author of more than twenty-five books. Known for his gift of illustration with words, Exley has often been referred to as the  "Norman Rockwell of writing." After serving churches in Colorado, Texas, and Oklahoma for the past twenty-six years, he now devotes his full time to writing and speaking.

When Richard is not speaking at retreats and conferences across the country, he and his wife, Brenda Starr, spend their time in a secluded cabin overlooking picturesque Beaver Lake. Richard enjoys quiet talks with old friends, kerosene lamps, good books, a warm fire when it is cold, and a good cup of coffee anytime. He's an avid Denver Broncos fan, an aspiring bass fisherman, and an amateur photographer.

For additional information on seminars, scheduling speaking engagements, or to write the author, please address your correspondence to:

Richard Exley
P. O. Box 54744
Tulsa, Oklahoma 74155

or call: 918-459-5434

or visit: **www.richardexleyministry.org**

ENDNOTES

1. Luke 8:50.

2. 1 Peter 5:5-7.

3. William L. Lane, *The Gospel of Mark: The New International Commentary on the New Testament* (Grand Rapids: William B. Eerdmans Publishing Company, 1974), p.192.

4. Leviticus 15:19-30.

5. Leviticus 20:18.

6. Matthew 8:2-4.

7. Luke 7:11-17.

8. Mark 5:25.

9. Leviticus 15:19-30.

10. G. Campbell Morgan, *The Great Physician*, (Old Tappan: Fleming H. Revell Company), p. 170.

11. Philip Yancey, "Helping Those in Pain" (*Leadership Journal*/84, Spring Quarter), p. 91.

12. Ibid.

13. Mark 5:26.

14. Mark 5:28.

15. Mark 5:27-29.

16. See 1 Corinthians 12:7-11.

17. Mark 5:27.

18. Mark 5:34.

19. Leviticus 20:10; Deuteronomy 22:20-24.

20. The Romans reserved the right of capital punishment to themselves.

21. John 8:11.

22. John 1:29.

23. Lamentations 3:22-23 (NRSV).

24. Romans 5:8.

25. Psalm 103:8,10-12,17.

26. Luke 13:10-17.

27. Luke 7:48.

28. Among the Jews it was a shameful thing for a woman to let her hair down in public, and only loose women did so. See Norval Geldenhuys, *The New International Commentary on the New*

Testament, *The Gospel of Luke* (Grand Rapids: William B. Eerdmans Publishing Company, 1979), p. 236.

29 Luke 15:4-7.

30 Luke 15:4.

31 James S. Stewart, *The Wind of the Spirit* (Nashville and New York: Abingdon Press, 1968), pp. 143-144.

32 2 Corinthians 5:17-18.

33 Thayer and Smith, *The KJV New Testament Greek Lexicon,* "Greek Lexicon entry for Bethesda," available from http://www.biblestudytools.net/Lexicons/Greek /grk.cgi?number=964&version=kjv.

34 John 5:2-3 (NKJV).

35 John 5:4 (NKJV).

36 John 5:1,9.

37 See John 5:16-18.

38 John 5:5.

39 John 9:1-3; Luke 13:1-5.

40 John 5:14.

41 Acts 9:1-21.

42 1 Timothy 1:15.

43 1 Timothy 1:16 (TLB).

44 Hebrews 4:15.

45 John 5:8-9.

46 John 5:14-15.

47 John 5:15.

48 John 5:16-18.

49 J. Wallace Hamilton, *Where Now Is Thy God?* (Old Tappan: Fleming H. Revell Company, 1969), p. 47.

50 Ephesians 3:20-21.

51 Leon Morris, *The Gospel According to John, The New International Commentary on the New Testament* (Grand Rapids: William B. Eerdmans Publishing Co., 1984), p. 274.

52 John 4:17-18.

53 2 Corinthians 5:17.

54 See Mark 3:7-12.

55 Matthew 19:26.

56 Luke 4:40.

57 Mark 1:27 (NKJV).

58 Luke 7:11-16.

59 Mark 5:35-42; Luke 8:49-56.

60 John 11:38-44.

61 Luke 24:1-6.

62 Matthew 15:26.

63 Matthew 15:27.

64 Matthew 15:28.

65 Hebrews 11:6.

66 Hebrews 13:8.

67 Matthew 7:11.

68 Isaiah 49:15-16 (NKJV).

69 *Matthew Henry, Matthew Henry Complete Commentary on the Whole Bible,* "Commentary on Isaiah 49," available from <http://bible.crosswalk.com/Commentaries/MatthewHenryComplete/mhc com.cgi?book=isa&chapter=049>. 1706.

70 Luke 12:32 (NKJV).

71 See Proverbs 19:17.

72 See Psalm 41:1.

73 Matthew 11:4-5.

74 John 7:46.

75 John 7:31.

76 John 7:42.

77 John 9:2.

78 Leon Morris, *The New International Commentary on the New Testament, The Gospel According to John* (Grand Rapids, MI: William B. Eerdmans Publishing Co., 1971), p. 478.

79 Ibid.

80 See 2 Corinthians 5:17.

81 John 9:3.

82 Arthur Gordon, *A Touch of Wonder* (Old Tappan: Fleming H. Revell Company, 1974), p. 89.

83 John 2:15-16.

84 John 2:23.

85 John 8:48,52.

86 John 7:51.

87 John 19:38-42.

88 Donald Miller, *Searching for God Knows What* (Nashville: Thomas Nelson, Inc., 2004), p. 83.

89 See Genesis 3:1-24; Romans 5:12-19.

90 Miller, op. cit., p. 84.

91 Ibid., p.44.

92 Romans 5:8.

93 Romans 10:9-13.

94 John 3:18.

95 Based on an account in James Bryan Smith, *Rich Mullins: An Arrow Pointing to Heaven* (Nashville: Broadman and Holman Publishers, 2000), pp. 57–58.

96 Luke 22:47-48.

97 Psalm 41:9.

98 Matthew 26:67.

99 Isaiah 50:6.

100 Isaiah 52:14.

101 Luke 23:35.

102 Psalm 22:7-8.

103 John 10:15,18.

104 Matthew 16:21.

105 Psalm 22:18.

106 Isaiah 53:2-3,5-6,10-12.

107 Isaiah 9:6-7.

108 Daniel 7:14.

109 Isaiah 7:14.

110 Micah 5:2.

111 Matthew 2:13-15.

112 Hosea 11:1; Matthew 2:19-21.

113 Isaiah 53:3; John 1:11.

114 Deuteronomy 21:22-23; Galatians 3:13; Zechariah 13:6.

115 Psalm 16:10; 49:15; Matthew 28:5-7; Acts 2:25-32.

116 Isaiah 9:7; Matthew 26:64.

117 Daniel 7:13-14,27.

118 Zechariah 13:6.

119 Luke 24:32.

120 For further study I would suggest Dr. Tim LaHaye's book *Jesus: Who Is He?* in which he lists many of the Messianic prophecies and their

fulfillment. Another great resource is *The Case for Christ* by Lee Strobel.

[121] Isaiah 7:14; Matthew 1:20-25.

[122] Micah 5:2.

[123] Isaiah 61:1-2; Luke 4:16-21.

[124] Psalm 41:9; Luke 22:47-48.

[125] Deuteronomy 21:22-23; Zechariah 13:6; Galatians 3:13.

[126] Lee Strobel, *The Case for Christ* (Grand Rapids: Zondervan Publishing House, 1998), p. 183.

[127] Ibid.

[128] Luke 24:25-27.

[129] John 1:14 (NRSV).

[130] Bob Benson and Michael W. Benson, *Disciplines for the Inner Life*, "Now and Then" by Frederick Buechner (Waco, TX: Word Books, 1985), p. 120.

[131] Deuteronomy 13:6-10,5.

[132] Acts 7:55,56.

[133] Acts 7:60.

[134] See Acts 20:23-24.

[135] Acts 13:9.

[136] Lloyd J. Ogilvie, *The Communicator's Commentary: Acts* (Waco: Word Books, Publisher, 1983), p. 208.

[137] Ephesians 2:4-10.

[138] 1 Timothy 1:13-16.

[139] See 1 Corinthians 11:27-29.

[140] See 1 Corinthians 11:23-26.

[141] Ogilvie, op. cit., p. 164.

[142] John 2:1-11.

[143] John 9:1-38.

[144] Luke 8:43-47.

[145] Luke 7:11-17.

[146] Matthew 17:1-8.

[147] John 21:25.

[148] John 1:14.

[149] Mark 4:35-41.

[150] John 11:33-44.

[151] John 13:14.

152 1 John 4:21.
153 1 John 3:18.
154 Daniel 7:9-14.
155 Matthew 17:1-8.
156 Acts 1:9-11.
157 Revelation 5:12.
158 Revelation 5:13.
159 Revelation 7:9-10
160 Revelation 7:14-17.
161 1 Corinthians 15:24-26,28.
162 Genesis 37:11-36.
163 Genesis 39:7-20.
164 Genesis 45:3-8.
165 Exodus 1:22; 2:3.
166 Exodus 2:5-10; Acts 7:18-22.
167 Philippians 1:12.
168 Philippians 1:6.
169 Revelation 1:17.
170 See Luke 21:26.
171 See Hebrews 13:5.
172 Hebrews 13:6.
173 See Exodus 3:7-8.
174 Revelation 11:15.
175 See 2 Corinthians 4:16-18.
176 See Revelation 15:4.
177 Daniel 2:44-45.
178 Revelation 21:3-4.

Additional copies of this book and other titles by Richard Exley
are available from your local bookstore.

If this book has touched your life, we would love to hear from you.
Please write us at:
editorialdept@whitestonebooks.com

"...To him who overcomes
I will give some of the hidden manna to eat.
And I will give him a white stone,
and on the stone a new name
written which no one knows
except him who receives it."
REVELATION 2:17 NKJV

Visit our website at:
www.whitestonebooks.com

WHITE STONE BOOKS
LAKELAND, FLORIDA